VOCATIONS ANONYMOUS

Vocations Anonymous

© 1996 by Sr. Kathleen Bryant, RSC, D. Min. All rights reserved

No part of this book may be reproduced in any written, electronic, recording, or photocopying without written permission of the publisher or author. The exception would be in the case of brief quotations embodied in the critical articles or reviews and pages where permission is specifically granted by the publisher or author.

Although every precaution has been taken to verify the accuracy of the information contained herein, the author and publisher assume no responsibility for any errors or omissions. No liability is assumed for damages that may result from the use of information contained within.

Books may be purchased by contacting the publisher at:

Rogationist Publications
6635 Tobias Ave.
Van Nuys, CA 91405
www.vocationsandprayer.org
vocationsanonymous@rogationists.org

ISBN: 978-0-9903469-0-6
1. Religion 2. Vocations 3. Discernment

First edition 1996
Second edition 1997
Third Edition 2014

Printed in the United States of America

10 9 8 7 6 5 4 3

Also by Kathleen Bryant:

Discern: Mission and Ministry, a Parish Program for Lay Leaders

All for Love, a Journal for Young Adults in Discernment

On the Way to Priesthood, a Workbook for Men in Discernment

VOCATIONS ANONYMOUS
A Handbook for Adults Discerning Priesthood and Religious Life

Kathleen Bryant, RSC, D. Min.

ROGATIONIST PUBLICATIONS
Los Angeles - Rome - Guadalajara

TABLE OF CONTENTS

Foreword		2
Preface		4

PART I: IS IT MY IMAGINATION OR IS GOD CALLING ME? HOW WILL I KNOW?

Chapter one	The Call	9
Chapter two	A theology of vocation	27
Chapter three	Discerning the call	35

PART II: LIFESTYLES OF THE POOR, OBEDIENT AND CELIBATE

Chapter four	Religious life	75
Chapter five	Vows	89
Chapter six	Sexually alive and celibate	95

PART III: SEARCHING

Chapter seven	Fear of Failure	113
Chapter eight	How to explore religious orders and the diocesan priesthood	121
Chapter nine	The application process (What to expect)	143
Chapter ten	The trip to the psychologist	147
Chapter eleven	Accepting "no"	155

PART IV: SPECIFICS

Chapter twelve	It's all in the timing	161
Chapter thirteen	What has my culture got to do with it?	165
Chapter fourteen	The baby issue	173
Chapter fifteen	Developing a holistic spirituality	179
Chapter sixteen	Being a women in the Church	189
Chapter seventeen	My own vocation story	195

PART V: SPACE FOR PRAYER

Pray creatively	205
Methods for praying	207
Prayer exercises	217
Online resources	237
Resource bibliography	241
Bibliography	259

FOREWORD

Any person serious about discernment for religious life or priesthood will find this book, quite simply, a work of grace. Sister Kathy Bryant has produced a rich stew of reflections, exercises, resources and eminently practical tools to help a person do the serious work of discernment.

Sister Kathy is a woman of great discipline. She is a practical theologian, a seasoned teacher and vocation minister, a spiritual director, and an accomplished speaker and retreat leader. All those attributes combine to produce a book of such practical wisdom that one comes away from the reading amazed at the precision with which she approaches discernment. The reader will benefit from a rare and graced guide in Sister Kathy. She provides historical as well as contemporary contexts for understanding the applied nature of consecrated service to the Church. Further, she houses her reflections in the best of post-Vatican II ecclesiology and spirituality.

Perhaps the most serendipitous surprise in the book is that Sister Kathy's own person, her deep prayer life, her radically honest sharing of her own story emerge as among the most valuable resources she offers. She is a woman of grace and blessing and loving service, and her own story has the power to give others the confidence to listen for their own truth.

I have had the privilege of working with vocation and formation directors since 1978. As well, I have conducted thousands of intense behavioral vocational assessments with both men and women candidates for religious life and priesthood. Never have I encountered a more helpful compendium of tools, resources and practical advice than I have in this book. Moreover it is an extraordinary resource not only for candidates, but for their directors as well. Many of the prayer suggestions offered toward the end of the book could well provide a common agenda for candidates and their guides to share together.

For sure, this book could only have come from the mind and heart of one who is a person of deep prayer and holy intimacy. Rather than intimidating or overwhelming the reader, Sister Kathy's humble and helpful presentation conveys the confidence that honest discernment will go well for the reader too.

A few years ago, Sister Kathy and I led a week-long training for vocation directors, formation directors, and their superiors from across the South Pacific. At the conclusion of the workshop in lovely Sydney, Australia, one of the female provincial superiors approached me and said, "Wow! Listening to Kathy is like drinking from a fire hose! She has so much wisdom!"

And so, dear reader, be forewarned: there is a sea of wisdom and grace about to come your way!

Reverend Raymond P. Carey, Ph.D.
Archdiocese of Portland in Oregon
February 23, 2014

PREFACE

Vocations Anonymous: for the call that just won't go away! Frequently, I hear women and men admit that even though they had thought about becoming a priest, sister or brother – and had dismissed the idea – the attraction to a church vocation keeps coming back. Many of the young adults I have met over the years wanted to keep their discernment questions within tight circles of those who would understand; thus, anonymous! This book is designed as a manual to help just such people, those who are in the process of discerning God's will. Whether you are feeling confused and need direction, or feeling fairly sure about your vocation, there is something here to help you be better informed about religious life or priesthood and about all the factors that will influence your discernment process.

This book was first written in 1995 on a Thanksgiving weekend! I prayed that it would bear fruit. Initially published by the National Coalition for Church Vocations, which has since closed, I am grateful to the Rogationists and *Vocations and Prayer* for their commitment to publish this latest edition.

There are a variety of ways to use this book. Read it cover to cover and then return to chapters that draw you. Use it as a workbook over a longer period of time, sharing your insights and growth with a spiritual director or friend. Peruse the *table of contents* to find the answers to questions you have right now, or spend your time working through the prayer and journal exercises in Section V. *Vocations Anonymous* is meant to be a companion for your discernment journey in the current, sometimes difficult, climate for those discerning priesthood or religious life. These words are meant to support your efforts and make locating the people and resources you need for discernment a bit easier.

Most of the discernment material in the book is drawn from the Spiritual Exercises of St. Ignatius and the Ignatian School of Spirituality. My spirituality has been shaped and formed by many Jesuits whom I have read, met, been taught by and worked with in Zambia, Ireland, California and Wales. My congregation, the Religious Sisters of Charity, has from it beginnings been shaped and formed by Ignatian Spirituality. What I have written about discernment in this text originated either in the thoughts of St. Ignatius of Loyola, or, through years of influence by many Jesuits and Religious Sisters of Charity.

I am grateful to Wilkie Au, Fr. Robert Juarez, and Sr. Jane de Lisle, CSJ of Orange, California, for their professional assistance in reading this text, and for their supportive and critical comments. I would also like to thank my parents, Frank and Patricia, now deceased, who through their deep faith and energizing joy, taught me to love God in an exciting and meaningful way. Double gratitude goes to Fr. Robert Juarez who retyped and edited the entire first edition since I did not have a digital copy.

May this manual enthuse you about the vocation to which God is calling you, so that you, too, may experience loving God in an exciting and meaningful way!

VOCATIONS ANONYMOUS

PART I

IS IT MY IMAGINATION OR IS GOD CALLING ME? HOW WILL I KNOW?

VOCATIONS ANONYMOUS

Chapter one

THE CALL

For over twenty years, I worked as a Talent Scout for God. I was one of the Vocation Directors for the Archdiocese of Los Angeles. I listened to young adults who struggled with a desire to give their lives to God and the church and were not sure if they had a calling to become a woman religious, brother, or priest. I took the phone calls, read the emails they sent and accompanied many of them as they journeyed through a process to discover their life calling.

I met some wonderful people who are now vowed religious and ordained priests. I also met people who were looking for a way to escape life instead of a way to embrace life. One day a woman phoned me insisting that she had a "calling." Upon inquiry, I discovered that she heard voices, was calling from a pay phone, and not quite sure to which parish she belonged. I learned quickly that a sign of a church vocation is desire to serve and the evidence in one's life that one is involved in some form of service or parish ministry. Other signs are that the young adult belongs to a parish community, has a personal relationship with God, healthy peer friendships, and age appropriate responsible behaviors – works or studies and pays their bills!

How do you know if you're called? What is the "calling"? Do you have to be saintly? Do you have to have certainty and clarity? Do you have to hear voices? Or like Moses see a burning bush?

Most of the young adults I have worked with, who entered the seminary or formation program in a religious order, described a very gentle invitation that kept coming up in their lives and "tempted" them to think about priesthood or religious life. This gentle call is not dramatic. It is not violent. It does not contradict their present value system. Often, people describe a thought that keeps recurring. During high school it was a fleeting hope. A few times during college perhaps they considered it again. Many young adults I met experienced the call more persistently after they achieved the "American Dream." They earned the BA or MBA; began climbing the corporate ladder or settling into the job they thought they always wanted. They have the condo and the car – and end up wanting "something more." That "more" is often described as a call. The most frequently heard descriptions of this call include a sense that "I want to be more," or "I want to give more."

One telltale sign of being called to "more" is that the hour of parish ministry or service is more life-giving and enjoyable than the forty or eighty hour work week! In ministry the person feels more authentically who he or she is really meant to be.

A "vocation" encompasses three distinct callings or aspects in our lives:

- Who the Lord calls *us to be*

- How the Lord call us *to become* ourselves in God (spirituality)

- What the Lord calls us *to do* for God and for others (ministry)[1]

_____

[1] Nemeck, Francis Kelly and Coombs, Marie Theresa. *Called by God, a theology of vocation and lifelong commitments.* Michael Glazier. Collegeville, MN: The Liturgical Press, 1992. p.2.

THE CALL

In a lighthearted effort to help people discover this "call" I have written a Vocation Anonymous Test. In no way do I want to denigrate any of the wonderful 12-Step programs that have become part of our contemporary spirituality. In my experience of walking with people through the vocation discernment process, there seems to be some commonalities between their experience and the characteristics of the 12 steps. In the early stages of vocation discernment, men and women want to remain anonymous. The thought of a priestly or religious vocation will not go away. It is something they have no control over. And so, just as AA has a questionnaire to determine if one may be an alcoholic, I devised some questions that may point out a church vocation.

VOCATIONS ANONYMOUS

Vocation Anonymous Test

Answer "yes" or "no" to the following questions:

YES	NO	Question
		Do you hide your vocation literature so no one will see you have it? Delete your browsing history on your computer in case someone else sees your exploration of religious communities?
		Does the idea of becoming a sister, priest or brother keep coming back time and time again even though you thought you had moved on in your life and forgotten about it?
		Do you feel called to give more, to be more?
		Does your relationship with God sustain you, enliven you, and invigorate you in such a way that you want to share the Good News with others?
		Do you find your weekly ministry more life-giving and energizing than your 40 or 60 hour work week?
		Do you long for "MORE"?
		Do you have a sneaking suspicion that you are on the brink of a major life decision?
		Are you afraid to tell friends and family that you are thinking about a church vocation?
		Does the idea of becoming a priest or religious excite you and at the same time frighten you because you feel "unworthy"?

THE CALL

(If you answered "yes" to two or more questions, email or call your local diocesan vocation office or the National Religious Vocation Conference, (773) 363-5454, www.nrvc. net to find a local contact person). Use the internet to explore, make friends on Facebook (National Religious Vocation Conference), and read blogs of religious and priests (A Nun's Life with blog and podcast).

The word vocation comes from the Latin *vocare*, to call. Implicit in this call is freedom. An invitation leaves the person free to say "yes" or "no." God invites us and never coerces. A vocation is a free invitation from God. There is no pressure, coercion, or manipulation. That is not to say that God won't try to "seduce" us. I have been seduced by God many times into doing something that I initially did not want to do. God has a way of inviting that sometimes is difficult to resist.

Remember the Old Testament passage from Jeremiah? "You seduced me, O Lord, and I let myself be seduced; you were too strong for me, and you triumphed. All the day I am an object of laughter; everyone mocks me. Whenever I speak, I must cry out, violence and outrage is my message; The word of the Lord has brought me derision and reproach all the day. I say to myself, I will not mention him, I will speak in his name no more. But then it becomes like fire burning in my heart, imprisoned in my bones; I grow weary holding it in, I cannot endure it" (Jeremiah 20: 7 – 9).

As you meditate on this passage, get in touch with your own experience of being loved by God. Does it move you to want to share that love with others? Is it like a fire burning in your heart and that you can't hold within yourself?

In Luke's Gospel, when Mary is called she is startled by the greeting and the invitation. Mary asks questions. "How

13

can this happen?" Mary knows who she is. "I am the servant of the Lord." Her "yes" comes out of a freedom. Mary embraces God's action in her life, her vocation. "Let it be done to me as you say." The Lucan account speaks of her being "deeply troubled" and asking questions. Yet, after her "yes" Mary skips, leaps off to her cousin Elizabeth singing a song proclaiming God's greatness.

I have seen this happen in many people's lives through vocation ministry. Initially they are disturbed by the thought that maybe God is really calling them. They ask questions. In discernment, they go deeper to discover who they really are. When they respond generously with a "yes" they experience a joy and peace that rings like Mary's Magnificat of Praise (see Luke 2).

Some men and women go through the discernment process and discover a call to marriage or to the single life. Because they too were open and generous with God and true to themselves, they experience the same joy and peace. It is the *unanswered* invitation that drives people nuts!

It is not easy to know where you are called. God wants to leave us free to respond so the invitation is gentle. If God were to dramatically intrude into our lives, we would not have the freedom to honestly respond. We would be knocked off kilter! In a wonderful book for discernment, *Addiction and Grace*, there is a description about this God who leaves us free.

God remains somewhat hidden in our lives, not only because of intimate immanence and awesome transcendence, but also because of a loving refusal to become another object of attachment. It would not be freedom to stand face to face with certainty before the God of creation and say yes to "Follow me." Who would say no? Further this "Follow me" is only a natural consequence of God's more primary request, "Love me." How could true, flowing love be born unless we freely choose the Lover, just as the Lover has first chosen us?[2]

The call is personal. No one "hears" the call the same way. You are "called by name" (Isaiah 43: 1). "Name," in the Old Testament culture, has a meaning beyond our arbitrary titles and names. Among the Hebrews, "name" signified the nature, essence and destiny of a person or thing. To name someone or something was an act of power and dominion. Recall the Genesis story when God gave the first couple the task of naming the animals (Genesis 2: 13 – 20). To "call by name" gave the one calling power over the other person. The psalmist says that we are called from our mother's womb. Modern medical technology allows us to discover characteristics of the unborn child, the nascent identity of the person who will become "name," in a way the psalmist never dreamed!

When I lived in the south central African nation of Zambia, I often felt close to Old Testament culture and values. Among Zambians a name was very important. In the Tonga tribe, a wife never called her husband by his first name. People were assigned names describing some characteristic. Soon after I began teaching in a Zambian public high school, the faculty gave me a new name. They called me "Sr. Namoonga" which was a clan of the Tonga tribe. This was an embracing, welcoming gesture. The students gave me my first name, "Choolwe," which means "lucky, happy, blessed." They saw me bouncing around, excited to be in Zambia, and gave me this new name. For five years, I was called Sister Choolwe Namoonga. I felt privileged and accepted with the gift of this name.

---

[2] May, Gerald. *Addiction and Grace.* New York; Harper and Row, 1988, p. 116.

This experience of being named reminded me that God often changed the names of people he called for a new task. Abram became Abraham, the father of a multitude. Simon became Peter. Throughout my life as a sister my name was changed several times according to the life I was called to live. The name changes have reflected often the change in convent culture, values, and my ministry. When I entered as a postulant, I was Sr. Bryant. As a novice, I was Sister Mary Joseph Bryant (Sr. MJB!). The Second Vatican Council called us to return to an awareness of Baptism as the origin of our vocations and so we religious were invited to return to using our baptismal name. I became Sr. Kathleen, then moved into a convent with three other "Sr. Kathleens"! When the elementary students would phone the convent, they would ask for the "old" Sr. Kathleen, the "fat" Sr. Kathleen, or the "young" Sr. Kathleen. To differentiate, I became Sr. Kathy. When I went to Ireland, Sr. Kathy sounded a whole lot different with the Dublin accent! When I went to Africa, it was Sr. Namoonga. I travelled to Vietnam twice and was privileged to be called Sr. Kim Binh by that community! Now I'm back to my Baptismal name and the one my family calls me.

In your own discernment, it might be helpful to reflect on your life's story and list all the names you have been called. For some, that may be an unpleasant task! List all the childhood and family nicknames, titles, friends' and lovers' names for you, and positions at work or school that may have given you a title. Is there any connection between the names and your own development? What names does God call you? In Isaiah 43, God calls you by name: "You are mine."

Given that "name" has this significance in scripture, being called by name means that you are called to be, first and foremost, that unique person God calls you to be. You are called as you are, not as you would hope you could be. God calls you by your name, with your unique personality, temperament, gifts, talents, weaknesses, and personal history. There is a freedom in that call. To know that you are called and loved as you are at this moment, gives you the space you need to listen to the call.

God Calls the Imperfect!

When I entered the convent in 1967, I was always in trouble for laughing too loud, talking too much, and moving too fast. I didn't have the "nun walk" or the "nun talk." I faced a few crises over who I was and how God could call me with all my flaws and weaknesses. I may have flunked "nun etiquette," but I have been very happy as a sister and ministered well in spite of it!

Being called is not a career; it is a lifelong vocation. A vocation is a call to love, to grow into the best self you can be, and into union with God. One of the finest definitions of a vocation is that by James and Evelyn Whitehead. They define "vocation" as a *conversation* with God.

A vocation is not a once-and-for-all call in young adulthood (to follow this career or enter this particular lifestyle). It is a lifelong conversation with God. Like any rich conversation, it is a patterned by periods of spiritual exchange, times of strain and argument, and intervals of silence. In such a developmental vision of a vocation, fidelity entails more than recalling an earlier invitation; it requires that we remain in the conversation. Our fidelity must be mobile because the conversation continues.[3]

---

[3] Whitehead, Evelyn and James. *Seasons of Strength*. Garden City, NY: Doubleday, 1944.

What is so exciting about this image is that God continues to call us throughout our lives. Being faithful means we are ready to listen and ready to respond to the twists and turns of our vocation that lie ahead. It is an active, creative, imaginative journey of fidelity.

Our particular vocation is rooted in our baptismal call. A call to be a priest or religious is not an "extra" call added to our baptismal call. It is not that priests or religious get the fancy frosted cake and the other "ordinary" Catholics called to marriage and single life get the plain version! It is crucial that vocation is understood in the context of Baptism because this sacrament is the foundation for the way priests and religious approach their ministry. A call comes from the community and for the community. If God has called you to be a priest, sister or brother, that call should echo from your parish community. Would the people who know you in your parish encourage you and support you in the call you discern? Would those with whom you work, socialize or minister support you?

If a person perceived their call to the priesthood or religious life as one that makes them "better" or "holier" than the rest of humankind, then it will be reflected in their attitudes, lifestyle and ministry. This contradicts the baptismal origin of call that we all share; a call that draws *all* people to holiness. We can always reflect on Jesus' sense of himself and his mission. Jesus served with humility and love; he identified himself in relationship to God. "The attitude you should have is the one that Christ Jesus had: He always had the nature of God, but he did not think that by force he should try to become equal to God. Instead of this, of his own free will he gave up all he had and took the nature of a servant" (Philippians 2: 5 – 7)[4]. Jesus never forgot that he

---

[4] *Good News Bible,* Catholic Study Edition, Thomas Nelson Publishers.

had been called "my Beloved Son" (Luke 3: 22).

Where do people experience God's call? I think it is very interesting to glance over some of the calls in Scripture and notice where people were and what they were doing at the time God called them. They were sleeping (1 Samuel 3: 1 – 18), fishing (Luke 5: 1 – 11), homemaking (Luke 1: 26 – 28), or tending sheep (1 Samuel 16: 1 – 13). They were doing ordinary things and heard God speak. We don't have to save money and take a trip to a shrine overseas to hear God speak. If we are attentive in our daily lives, in our most ordinary tasks, we will meet God.

Excuses, Excuses!

Are you in a panic by now? Afraid that maybe you really *do* have a vocation to priesthood or religious life? A few excuses might be handy. The most common excuses that I have heard in vocation ministry are:

1. I am not holy enough.

2. I'm afraid I'll fail.

3. I've made mistakes; I'm a sinner.

4. I'm not talented enough.

5. I don't feel comfortable with all the stances of the institutional Church.

6. I'm from a dysfunctional family.

7. I could never stand up and speak in front of a crowd!

8. I'm afraid of making a permanent commitment.

Notice that in every excuse, all the attention is on the

self. This is a sure fire plan for disaster! Well, you are in good company. You aren't alone in your fears. There are stories of men and women in the Bible who also tried to resist God's call through excuses. Perhaps you can identify with some of them.

"I'm too young!" – Jeremiah

"I can't speak…I stutter…ask my brother." – Moses

"How can this happen to me?" – Mary, Mother of Jesus

"Lord, leave me. I'm a sinful man." – Peter

"Ha! At my age?"…chuckle, chuckle – Sarah

Let's run through those excuses again.

I'm not holy enough. Who is? No one is *worthy* of God's attention and love, of Baptism, of a church vocation. Everything is a pure gift from God. We do not "merit" or "earn" God's love!

I'm afraid I'll fail. Explore these feelings of failure. Do you think Jesus ever feared taking the next step? If we are paralyzed by fear of failure, what would we ever do? Another consideration is that perhaps the worst thing is not failure. It could be part of God's plan. Jesus' life looked like a failure.

I've made mistakes. I'm a sinner. Who hasn't sinned? Who isn't a sinner?

I'm not talented enough. It's like the multiplication of the loaves. You offer God what you have and you watch it transformed into the gifts you need for ministry.

I don't feel comfortable with all the stances of the institutional Church. Do you think that St. Martin de Porres, the mixed-race Peruvian slave who doctored and fed the poor of Lima, was comfortable with the institutional Church's position on slavery? There are great saints who challenged the institutional Church during their lifetimes, and great Catholics today who do the same. There is a prophetic dimension to our Catholic tradition.

I'm from a dysfunctional family. It is said that 60% – 90% of those in the priesthood and religious life, those in discernment and formation come from dysfunctional families. You're in good company. Apart from the personal work you need to do on issues coming from such a family background, you will also recognize that you have sensitivities and certain gifts from your experience that will enable you to minister well pastorally.

I could never stand up and speak in front of a crowd. Many priests and religious thought the same thing! Look at them now!

I'm afraid of making a permanent commitment. Seminary and initial formation programs give you the time and space to really see if priesthood or religious life fit before you make any kind of commitment. Remember the quote from the Whiteheads about a vocation being conversation. If you stay in the conversation, no matter what twists and turns it takes, you will be faithful in the end to whatever commitment you are called to live out.

Real temptations face the person called. You might wonder, "If only…I was more intelligent, gifted and had more discipline. If only I weren't so shy, so independent…"

The best way to counteract temptation is to do what Jesus did. When He was tempted three times in the desert Jesus responded with three different Scripture texts. In time of personal struggle, use the communal, sacred texts for prayer. "Here I am, Lord, I come to do you will" (Psalm 40: 7 – 8). "With God all things are possible" (Luke 1: 37).

Another temptation might be to escape God. Remember

the story of Jonah running off in the opposite direction after having been called? (Jonah 1: 3). Where do you run to?
What forms of escape do you take? Some people just get
busier when they sense God calling. Others escape through
movies, food, compulsive exercise, books, or gathering advice from everyone instead of taking time to listen to God.

If you are tempted to think you are not good enough,
then counteract that thought with a focus on your best self.
You, like all people, are *in the process* of becoming day by
day the person God created you to be. It is a process. What
we feed our minds in terms of our self concept will affect
who we become. If you give up on yourself before the process is complete, you will never discover what it means to be
fully alive.

Another temptation is to copy another person's process
of discernment or way to God. You cannot use the same
vocation discernment timeline as another person. Some
people enter seminary in high school; others enter at age 50.
Some people discern in 6 months that God is calling them
to religious life or priesthood; others spend a couple of years
discerning. When a person copies the lifestyle and actions
of Saint "Whoever," it is often out of insecurity of a lack of
sense of self. God does not ask you to live exactly like St.
John of the Cross or St. Therese of Lisieux. You are called
to be you! Your first vocation is to be yourself as a person
created in God's image; to be faithful in the context of this
particular time, place and culture. In sacred scripture, we
read how God called disciples through ordinary events. Today God may speak on the freeway, while you're handing
out food at a Soup Kitchen, at the gym, or at the Hollywood
Bowl during a concert. We may do violence to ourselves by
trying to force who we are into another person's mold or try
to imitate their way to God.

THE CALL

The challenge is to live out a call, to work out salvation in the circumstances of this particular time and place *now* as opposed to "if only," or "wait until…" Even though it is not clear and defined, I am called to live out my call in the present moment as I am. If Jesus had to wait for the next step and listen to his Father, then we must wait and listen as well. How did Jesus know when to move away from home, begin his mission, heal this person, or challenge the other? Jesus listened and responded. This is authentic obedience. Allow God to use you by being your honest self.

The next chapter will help you to situate your call authentically in the context of church teaching and theology.

First Steps – or – What to do when you experience that gentle invitation!

When you first begin to think about priesthood or religious life, it can be frightening! It is difficult to know where to begin. What would be a safe place to start? Who can you trust with this thought? Here are some suggestions for the very first steps in checking out your vocation.

1. **Pray!**

   In a very intentional and conscious way, open yourself up to God's presence. God is bombarding us with blessings and presence everywhere and at all times; but we are often closed. Relax…open up…give God some quality time. If the recommendation for good health is a minimum of 20 minutes of exercise three times a week, then spend a similar amount of time listening to God for your spiritual health.

   If you have not spent much time praying and are unsure about how to begin, there are some suggestions for prayer in the final section of this book, *Space for Prayer*. You might want to take some time with this section as you read through the book. Occasionally in the text you'll be notified when an exercise in that section might be particularly helpful.

2. **Get a notebook**

Start writing down what you experience. When did you first notice this call? What comments, encouragement, or invitation have others given you to consider it? What "nudges" has God given you?

Are there any particular events that started you thinking about a vocation to priesthood or religious life? Are there any scripture texts that struck you to the core?

3. **Remember**

Recall your personal faith history. Where have you been? When did you first experience God? How has your image of God changed since you were a child?

4. **Talk to someone you can trust**

Talk to one person. In the early stages of vocation discernment, don't tell your family and friends. They may start treating you differently and not give you the freedom to genuinely discern your call.

5. **Start looking around**

Gently, start looking around at the priests and religious you have known.

Pick up your local Catholic newspaper, magazine or directory to notice ads for vocation events, retreats and other activities. Browse the web and Google to learn more. You might email some contacts you find. There are plenty of Vocation websites.

THE CALL

6. **Get involved**

Get involved in some form of service or parish ministry (teaching a religious education class, serving as a lector, minister of the Eucharist, visiting the elderly, feeding the homeless, etc.).

7. **Enlist the support of prayerful people**

Ask people to pray for you. You don't have to specify an intention. You could suggest that you are trying to discover God's will for your life, or that you are trying to make a decision. Consider asking prayer from your family, close friends, a prayer group at the parish, a rosary group or cloistered contemplative men or women. (Call them on the phone and ask!)

8. **Pay attention!**

Notice and pay attention to what is life-giving and energizing for you. What "sparks" fly out at you in your life? Where's the passion? The attraction?

Write any incidents, relationships, scripture texts, etc. in your notebook that enliven you. They are all pointers and clues.

VOCATIONS ANONYMOUS

Chapter two

A THEOLOGY OF VOCATION

Do you have a vocation?

We *all* have a vocation! Each baptized person has a vocation to become like Christ, a call to holiness.[5] The Second Vatican Council brought us back to a renewed sense of our baptismal call. Before the Council, a "vocation" was associated only with sisters, priests and brothers. If you were married or single, it was not considered as "high" or "holy" a vocation. Since the Council, the Church has come to an appreciation of the value of each vocation: the single life, married vocation, priesthood and religious life. No one call is a holier vocation, only that one to which you live out your call to holiness.

"The whole Church is called and sent into the world to continue the mission of Jesus with the force of the Spirit: the People of God, established by Christ as a fellowship of life, charity, and truth is also used by God as an instrument for the redemption of all, and is sent forth into the world as the light of the world and salt of the earth."

"The whole Church is constituted in a *state of vocation and of mission*, and therefore each member of the Church, each for his own part, is constituted in a state of vocation and of mission. Each one, by virtue of the common priesthood of the People of God, cooperates in the mission of the

---

[5] *Lumen Gentium. The Documents of Vatican II.* NY: Guild Press. 1966. #39 – 42 "All of Christ's followers, therefore, are invited and bound to pursue holiness."

Church, through the profession of faith, through evangelization, through participation in the Eucharist and the other sacraments, through prayer, through the testimony of life, through active charity and through the various forms of the apostolate."

"With this universal call to manifest the mission of the universal priesthood is linked the universal call to holiness in the path of the Lord Jesus, model and master of the whole Christian life."[6]

A vocation to be a priest, religious, single or married person is rooted in the same baptismal call. Religious were traditionally given a new name upon entering the novitiate and receiving the habit. Now in most communities, people retain their baptismal name as a sign that their vocation to priesthood or religious life is a unique invitation rooted in the baptismal call of all Christians.

A look at the Bible reveals some of the special tasks for which God chose women and men. In both the Old and New Testaments, God chose people to serve in a myriad of ways. Some were prophets, kings or queens, shepherds, married, single or widowed, old or young, rich or poor, prominent and marginalized.

Just like these biblical characters, each of us is called by name.[7] God takes the initiative. You don't "get" a vocation or call to priesthood. You are given, called, nudged, shaken, or get a wake up call by God. This call is given in freedom. We can say "No." This call is also personal. Our first vocation is to be ourselves through Christ in Baptism. The call develops as we grow in faith.

---

[6] *The Conclusive Document: developments of pastoral care for vocations in the local churches. Experiences of the past and programs for the future.* The international congress of bishops and others with responsibilities for ecclesial vocations. Synod Hall, Vatican. 1981. #8.

[7] Isaiah 43: 1

A THEOLOGY OF VOCATION

"God's call creates each of us into a unique person with a particular way to reach full maturity in Christ. We receive a singular identity as well as the potential to attain maximum development of our personhood. We receive the power to experience, to know and love the Lord. Integral to the Lord's calling us by name then is the mystery of our being and becoming in God."[8]

A call to priesthood comes through the local community, the local parish. If you read the Acts of the Apostles or accounts of the early Church, you will notice that the person who presided at the Eucharist was chosen from among the community.

The gifts of the Spirit are given for the good of the community. "What you have received, freely give."[9] Whatever special gifts or charisms we have received have been given for us to use in service to others. So a vocation to priesthood or religious life is a call from the local church for the Church.

The theology of a vocation flows from a theology of Church. The Church is not a building; it is a living organic reality. The Church is a sacrament of the risen Christ. This means that the Church is a sign of the Risen Jesus' presence and grace among us. When you pray in the name of Christ with two or three people, whether it is scriptural, liturgical, or spontaneous prayer, you are experiencing the Church. Through the Eucharist, the Church best expresses its role as the sacrament of Christ. By Eucharist, I don't mean solely receiving the Body and Blood of Christ, but also breaking open the Word of God, and the fellowship which ensues.

The Church is called to engage the world. The King-

---

[8] Nemeck and Coombs, p. 51.

[9] Matthew 10: 8

dom of God includes more than the Catholic Church. Just to clarify this point, remember that when the Kingdom is realized there will be no need for the Church. When Jesus speaks of the Kingdom of God, he includes more than all those good Catholics who have lived, died, and are yet to be born! Good Lutherans, Baptists, and Evangelicals are also part of the Kingdom of God! The saving power of God is not confined to Catholics.

As Church we are called to identify with the world and at the same time to be prophetic and eschatological. The Church prophetically challenges injustice, sin and the lack of truth that pervades our cultures. That is why the Church gets involved in the political, economic, social and cultural dimensions of life. If we are called to be Church, we are called to speak up as Jesus did for the poor and oppressed.

The Church is eschatological, meaning that it reminds us of the last things: death, judgment, heaven and hell. So the Church is always a reminder of what is to come that is not yet here, not yet realized. We are called to remind others that this is not all there is.

The Church sends people out on mission to the world so that the Kingdom may be further realized. We are strengthened, healed and fed by the sacraments. The local community that is built up through sacrament and service exists for the larger mission of Christ reaching out of the entire universe. The Church is Jesus' gift of himself to the world. As St. Teresa of Avila wrote,

"Christ has no body but yours."[10]

Christ has no body now but yours
No hands, no feet on earth but yours.
Yours are the eyes through which he looks
Compassion on this world.

[10] St. Teresa of Avila, "Christ Has No Hands."

Yours are the feet with which he walks to do good.
Yours are the hands with which he blesses all the world.

Yours are the hands
Yours are the feet
Yours are the eyes,
You are his Body.

Christ has no body now but yours
No hands, no feet on earth but yours.
Yours are the eyes through which he looks
Compassion on this world.
Yours are the feet with which he walks to do good.
Christ has no body on earth but yours.

Reflection

A person's theology of a vocation grows out of an understanding of the Church. Take a few minutes to reflect on your own vocation, the universal call to holiness that you experienced at your baptism. Have you ever reflected on your own baptismal call? Find out the details of your Baptism, especially if you were baptized as a baby. If you apply to a seminary or religious community, you will need a copy of your baptism certificate. Why not go ahead and get a copy? Sometimes it takes a while, especially if you were baptized in another country. Who are your godparents? Do your parents remember your baptismal day? You might want to pray with a photograph of your baptism.

Being called from the community. Has anyone in your parish encouraged you to consider becoming a priest, deacon, brother, or sister? Who thinks that you would make a good priest or religious? Have you ever checked it out with any of the parishioners you know?

It is extremely important in discernment that you be involved in some form of parish ministry or community service. Perhaps you teach in a religious education program or work in a soup kitchen. If you asked those who work with you about your sense of being called, what would they say?

Being called for the community. Do you envisage your vocation to be one that is intended for the service to others? The cloistered contemplatives that I know hunger to pray for the intentions of the world and of individuals. Their prayer lives are focused outwards on the needs of the community. Do you see your vocation as serving self or serving the community? Are you willing to work hard and expend yourself in the service of others? Is status or prestige a temptation for you in your consideration of priesthood and religious life?

Prophetic. "If you were arrested for being a Christian today, would there be enough evidence to convict you?" How and when do you take a stand in your life against injustice? Speak up? Write letters? Forms of protest?

Eschatological. What in your lifestyle proves that you live as if this is not all there is? Where does your hope lie?

Sacraments. How are community and parish celebrations a genuine part of your life? How have you experienced both personally and communally the presence of Christ in your midst through the sacraments?

The Kingdom. How do you embrace those of other faiths? Do you affirm any common ground? Do you speak out of any prejudice or ignorance about the Kingdom encompassing more than the Catholic Church?

As a future sister, priest or brother, how would you see your mission and ministry with reference to the wider community?

A THEOLOGY OF VOCATION

Does your social circle include those of different faith backgrounds?

Service. What gifts do you put at the service of the parish? Your family? Your city? Your campus? Your work?

These reflection questions can help you situate your call within a healthy sense of the Church. Which areas do you need to work on in your living of the Catholic faith?

The next chapter will help you move into the actual process of discernment.

VOCATIONS ANONYMOUS

Chapter three

DISCERNING THE CALL

How do you go about discovering God's will? Supposing that you suspect God may be calling you to priesthood or religious life, how do you go about getting more clarity? How do you find out?

The process of working out where you are called is called "discernment." The word discernment comes from the Latin word *discernere* which means to distinguish, to sift out, to separate what may be from God and what may come from egocentric interests or cultural pressures. Discernment is a process of listening to the inner movements and learning to sift out what is from God and what is not from God. Discernment is a choice between two goods. You don't discern between good and evil.

In his book *Weeds Among the Wheat*, Thomas Green relates discernment to Matthew's parable of the weeds among the wheat (Mt. 13: 24 – 30).[11] We are all a mixture of pure and impure motivations. We carry our own personal baggage into our prayer and our discernment.

To discern...

- Is to spend time listening;

- Is to admit that we are powerless over our own ability to

---

[11] Green, Thomas. *Weeds Among the Wheat: Where Prayer and Action Meet.* Notre Dame, IN: Ave Maria Press. 1984.

be certain, to be in control, to have all the answers;

- Is to set out on a journey with God, confident that we will be cared for, that we will have all we need, that we have nothing to fear (Psalm 23);

- Is to really live life by the choices we make and not allow ourselves to be the victims of circumstance. This means taking responsibility for the direction of my life, for the decisions I make and not blaming anyone else for my unhappiness;

- Is to actively cooperate with God in co-creating a future full of hope, meaning and promise (Jeremiah 29);

- Is to be alert, frightened, surprised, joyful and rooted (sometimes all at once);

The primary task of discernment is to sort out all your impulses, attractions, fantasies and desires. An image that might help is that of a spring cleaning campaign in the household of your psyche. You clean up both the attic and the basement. You come across all those things that you have stored up in your life and sometimes forgotten – memories in your hope chest, photos to remind you of your personal history, clothes that suit you and those you toss. You may decide to remodel the house. You may discover some "rooms" you will need now that you had no use for previously. You may spend a lot of time in the basement doing some basic ground work before you can begin discernment.

If you are out of touch with your affective side, you will want to do some basic work in acknowledging what you feel. If you have been careless in spending and have run up a debt, you will want to strategize about how you can become debt-free. If you have unresolved sexual identity issues you will want to get some information, talk to someone and work on negotiating your attitudes, responses and relationships.

Discernment is a lifelong task. It is not only a process you "use" in order to discover whether you should enter the convent or seminary, get married or remain single. As Catholic Christians who live in union with Christ, we want to respond freely to the Spirit and not be influenced by any whim, inclination, pressure from others, or media gimmick.

If you really believe that God loves you, you will experience a certain freedom in your life. If you know you are loved, you will grow in security. You can make choices. You won't be inhibited by what others may think of you because you are settled within yourself. You know who you are and trust yourself. We grow gradually into these self understandings. Being loved frees us to be open. Openness is a prerequisite for discernment.

Attitudes for Good Discernment

Openness means you will allow yourself to explore all of the possibilities for your life. You will short circuit the discernment process if you begin discernment with an obsession to become a priest or religious. How can you listen when you already have the answer?

In this model of discernment, St. Ignatius of Loyola recommends that we begin in a place where we are equally open to one choice as much as the other. He calls this "indifference." Indifference does not mean that we do not care. It means that we are so open to whatever God wants that one choice will be just as welcomed in our life as another. Remember, discernment is a choice between two goods. Through indifference, you are not open to a choice which is evil or immoral; you work towards openness between two goods.

VOCATIONS ANONYMOUS

To cultivate an attitude of openness, you might want to pray the prayer of abandonment by Charles de Foucauld, in Section V of this book. If you find it difficult to be truly open to whatever God asks, then pray for the desire to be open.

Another attitude necessary for discernment is trust. This trust is grounded in a faith that believes that God wants the best for you; more than you do! If you are tempted to research every catalogue there is on different religious orders, visit a multitude of convents or formation houses, and through your research make the best decision through your own power, you are operating on the assumption that you are in charge! Doing the "homework" is important only if it is in the context of faith. God calls. In an honest discernment process, you may lose control of the direction of the process. The outcome may be quite unexpected! Surrender, trusting that God will never lead you to a place where you will not be happy.

Relax!

God is the one leading and calling. In your trusting, learn to relax. A sister I know used to say that the devil is a tight diaphragm. There is a lot of wisdom in that. If you notice yourself growing tense, nervous and anxious in the discernment process, step back, breathe, and remember that this is not your doing!

Discernment is a process; therefore, it takes time. It is impossible to rush the growth of a living thing. Accept discernment as a process which takes time and necessarily goes through different phases of development. You will not move directly from doubt to clarity. You may not experience a consistent movement towards light. The process mirrors our lives. Although you are moving forward, sometimes it may feel like you have gone backwards.

Your discernment will be uniquely your own process. Don't try to copy someone else's discernment. There is no "right" age for God to call, no right time, no right sequence of tasks to discern properly. Honor your own personal history, rhythm and response to God.

Two images of the discernment process that may help are that of the garden and that of an expectant mother.

The Garden

If you have a garden or a plot of land that you want to be fruitful or beautiful, there is a process of preparing it and waiting for growth to occur. In Africa, there was a season in which the land was cleared by setting huge fires. The fires burned away the old growth. This practice reminded me of the Advent theme of clearing a way for God, smoothing out the rough ways. Part of discernment is clearing away, cleaning up, throwing out the clutter that may confuse the matter to be discerned. One way to do this on a personal level is maybe to clear away some unimportant, time-consuming activities to give quality time to your discernment. One woman, who eventually entered a contemplative order, took three months off from work to focus on her discernment. Not everyone has that luxury, but it is possible to set apart some quality time daily that otherwise may have been spent on some useless activity.

The notion of "space" is also vital in discernment – space in your life to discern, space to be yourself, space to make a free choice. Both Isaiah and John the Baptist challenge us to do this. You might want to ritualize this by setting apart a space in your bedroom, apartment or home to be sacred space, a prayer corner. You might want to clean out some "cupboards" and throw out what is not necessary to create space symbolically in your discernment for new concepts and possibilities. You can clear space in your calendar for discernment.

Plowing or preparing the earth for planting is physically demanding. I remember seeing people bent over in the fields with little hoes early in the mornings of the African cold season. The earth has to be loosened before anything can be planted. What is the hard, dry earth of your life? What can you do to loosen the soil? How can you soften the soil of your heart to receive the Word of God?

Planting is methodical, systematic, and attentive. Planting happens seed by seed. It demands patience and attention. It may be that your discernment process is a slow, steady attentiveness to passage after passage, experience by experience, sense and intuition.

After you do the plowing and the planting, the challenge is to wait for the rain. Trust that it will come. Rain could come in the form of a warm enthusiastic welcome in a community or diocese, a gut sense that the community you encounter matches your own hopes and dreams, or a quiet experience that confirms your sense of being called.

You are not safe yet! After the rains come signs of growth. Not all that grows is beautiful in your life. Discernment is the art of distinguishing the weeds from the wheat. You may have to do some weeding. The liturgical seasons of Advent and Lent invite us to do that inner weeding out of all that has crept up in our lives that is not of God.

Praise God for the growth. After all your work, waiting and hoping, acknowledge that the growth comes from God.

DISCERNING THE CALL

The Expectant Attitude

Discernment involves the waiting and hopefulness that carries a promise of new birth. A model for genuinely listening to God and faithfully responding is that of Mary. If you can divest yourself of the layers of devotion to Mary that may have cluttered the reality of this young woman's human struggles, you may discover that she faced challenges similar to your own. Mary experienced fear. Mary asked questions. Twice in the annunciation story, Mary is referred to as "virgin." In the social context of her time, the virginity of a woman meant *nonattachment*. She did not belong to anyone. In discernment, you need the spirituality of the virgin. Spiritual virginity signifies a radical dependence on God, and an independence, or detachment from any human being. The virgin is both open and empty, both independent and dependent.

Cultivating the emptiness of the virgin requires openness, detachment and readiness. This inner freedom is:

Like the hollow in a reed, the narrow riftless emptiness which can have only one destiny: to receive the piper's breath and to utter the song that is in his heart…an emptiness like the hollow in the cup, shaped to receive water and wine.[12]

"How will this happen?" Mary asks. Mary thinks that she must do something in order to give birth. The Angel tells her, on the contrary, that she must let something happen to her. When Mary opens herself to the power of the Most High, new possibilities of life will emerge. Mary responds, "Be it done to me according to Your word." As the Word takes flesh within her body, Mary begins nurturing the babe within her womb, waiting expectantly. In discern-

[12] Shannon, William H. *"Original Blessing: The Gift of the True Self."* The Way. 30:1. 1990. P. 42.

41

ment, we too are called to be open to new possibilities of a word becoming flesh in our lives. We are called to wait, to nurture new life and hope within us. We are called to focus, not on our fears and uncertainties, but on God's favor and delight in us. This awareness of God's love will give us the freedom to be open.

Mary refuses to give into the fear and confusion of having unanswered questions. Fear can close you down, pull you into yourself, cause you to shrink back. Instead of fear, Mary heard words of favor from the angel. Favor is for mission. Mary made the choice to move forward blessed with this sense of favor, rather than give in to the fear and the uncertainty before her. This choice gave her freedom and joy to move out toward another person, as she set out to visit Elizabeth.

Inner Freedom

A good barometer of your inner freedom is to imagine yourself giving God a blank check! Inner freedom means that you are so detached from your own ideas, possessions, relationships and attitudes that you will go anywhere and do anything if you come to discern that it is God's will for you to do so.

We are living in an age of rapid change and a multiplicity of options. The staggering technological changes of the last thirty years have had an impact on our daily life. Living with change challenges us to look at new models or paradigms of ministry. Without inner freedom, however, we will be unable to imagine new possibilities for life. Attachment to ideas, concepts, and opinions can block us off from God's spirit.

Freedom is frightening. We fear that if we give it all to

God, we will be somehow cheated, lose everything and end up being miserable. But when we let go, we gain. We gain joy! "True inner freedom is characterized by great unbounded love, endless creative energy, and a deep pervasive joy."[13]

God's Will

A few observations about God's will may help to alleviate some fears and unfounded beliefs. As I meet with women and men discerning a church vocation, occasionally I'll interview someone who says that "God has called" them to the priesthood or religious life. When I ask about their desires, it sometimes turns out that they have no desire, but only a compelling conviction that it is God's will. If there is no desire to be a priest or religious, how could that be an authentic call?

A vocation is from a community and for a community. If a person's awareness of call is only a "private revelation," and not affirmed by a community, how does that gel with a sense of baptismal and communal call? In addition to community affirmation, a sense of joy, peace, and life are signs of an authentic call. They are not the sole criteria, but an integral part of discernment and a sign that God's will is in harmony with your deepest desires.

Sometimes it can be a frustrating experience to discern God's will. Some young adults think of God's will as a big blueprint somewhere "up there." They might think, "if only I could just get a little peek of it," as if they had nothing at all to do with God's will as it unfolds in their lives. God's will is not a predetermined, laid out blueprint "out there" somewhere. God's will, the key to our future, lies in the desires of our hearts as they correspond to God's infinite goodness

[13] May, Gerald. *Addition and Grace*. New York: Harper and Row, 1988, p. 144.

and wisdom.

The word "salvation" means *well being*. Sometimes we have a fear of discovering God's will. What if it means pain? What if God's will means that I'll be miserable and suffer? Remember that God's will is our well being. If we are faithful in responding to God's will, then we will be the best self we can be, the most authentic self, the most genuinely joyful self. That's not to say we might not suffer pain. But the bottom line will be peace and joy.

All religion…is concerned to overcome fear. We can distinguish real religion from unreal by contrasting their formulae for dealing with negative motivation. The maxim of illusory religion runs: Fear not; trust in God and God will see that none of the things you fear will happen to you; that of real religion, on the contrary is: Fear not; the things that you are afraid of are quite likely to happen to you, but they are nothing to be afraid of.[14]

We believe that God desires a personal relationship with us and that Divine Providence, the wisdom at the heart of creation, is a reality in our lives. God, the One, the Mystery, the Divine Presence, is involved in every aspect of our lives and in the universe. God is both transcendent and immanent. Fr. John Powell, SJ, invites us to remember three premises before beginning a discernment process. Spend time with each of these statements in the silence of your heart and observe how it resonates with your faith.

- God loves me more than I love myself.

- God desires my happiness more than I do.

- God knows best how I'll be happy.

---

[14] McMurray, John. *Persons in Relation.* New York: Harper, 1957, p. 171. Gilford Lectures 1953 – 1954.

DISCERNING THE CALL

Do you believe these statements? How does this belief impact our feelings about God's will?

God is alive in you, acting from within your personal history. This God, who sustains you in being, sparks desires in you for something more. God breathes life into you as you imagine, reflect, laugh, create, dance, pray, and think.

Discernment engages the whole of your life. It is not a question of focusing on what happens during your prayer time only. If the paragraph above startled you and you noticed that prayer was listed pretty far along the list, could you see all of the activities listed as revelatory of God? Discernment involves every aspect of your life. The so-called "parts" of our lives are organically connected and interdependent. Your work, social life, physical and emotional wellbeing, and the intellectual development are all part of your spirituality. If you experience tension in your body, it is most likely related to how you work, relate, and cope. As you listen to how things are going at work, you may have a clue about discerning your future.

Discernment is a win/win situation. If you spend six months, a year or two years discerning, you will come out of it with a deeper faith, a better sense of yourself, a more intimate relationship with God, more knowledge about religious life or priesthood, and an understanding of the discernment process that will help you in future decisions.

I have never met a man or woman who went though discernment and found it a waste of time. I also have never met anyone who after spending a year or two in the seminary or in a formation program would not do it all over again, even though they discovered it was not the life for them.

45

Movements

As you struggle towards these attitudes of trust, openness and inner freedom, you will notice that there are tugs and pulls, attractions, inclinations, temptations and graces. We experience movements towards God, as well as counter-movements dragging us back towards selfishness, doubt and darkness. The raw material for any discernment are these movements at the affective level. We may experience affect as joy, fear, peace, anxiety, restlessness, boredom, or wonder. The feelings you experience can indicate something going on at a deeper level.

Discerning the spirits involve cutting through what you feel and think to the core dynamic which fuels your feelings and thoughts. Edwina Gately, founder of the Volunteer Missionary Movement, says that God lives about three inches in from the belly button!

If you are a person unaware or unable to name your feelings, you will want to do some work on this issue in order to genuinely discern. St. Ignatius' method of discernment honors and integrates both the rational (head) and affective (heart) realities of our makeup. You will not be able to observe a significant part of the process if you are not able to observe your feelings. There are programs which can enable you to begin naming and observing your affective life, especially if you are an adult child of a family with a dysfunctional background. A 12-step group known as Adult Children of Alcoholics (ACOA), have group meetings all over the country. If there is no way you could consider being challenged and growing in such a group, you might consider some counseling at the beginning of your discernment process that will enable you to be freed and more aware of affect.

Consolation

St. Ignatius gives names to the two movements we experience through affect. The movement that leads towards God he calls *consolation.* The counter-movement, he names *desolation.* A person experiences these movements throughout the day in various degrees.

Consolation is a state in which you feel peace at a deep level, even though you may be suffering or struggling. It is not an ecstatic feeling or "warm fuzzy." When in a state of consolation, a person is moved to greater faith and trust in God. A person could be in pain or grief, and yet, experience consolation from their faith in God. Consolation reflects a harmony between head and heart. Your guts and emotions are less able to manipulate your action. Your rational side does not repress your feelings. Consolation is much more than a superficial high. It runs deeper than the stresses and strains of daily life.

I call it consolation when an interior movement is aroused in the soul, by which it is inflamed with love of its Creator and Lord, and as a consequence, can love no creature on the face of the earth for its own sake, but only in the Creator of them all. It is likewise consolation when one sheds tears that move to the love of God, whether it be because of sorrow for sins, or because of the sufferings of Christ our Lord, or for any other reason that is immediately directed to the praise and service of God. Finally, I call consolation every increase of faith, hope and love, and all interior joy that invites and attracts to what is heavenly and to the salvation of one's soul by filling it with peace and quiet in its Creator and Lord.[15]

For those who are living a graced life, St. Ignatius com-

---

[15] St. Ignatius of Loyola, *Spiritual Exercises,* #316, Third Rule of the First Week.

pares the action of the Spirit to water falling on a sponge. This action is gentle, peaceful and comforting. The contrasting action of the evil one is like water falling on a stone, noisy, disruptive and disturbing.[16]

Desolation is a state in which you experience darkness, restlessness, boredom, discouragement, or despair. You may falter in your good intentions and habits and settle for the "less good." The danger of desolation is that a person settles for mediocrity. Imagine what the rich young man of the Gospel would say if you interviewed him thirty years after his encounter with Jesus!

St. Ignatius wrote the *Spiritual Exercises* out of his own experience of discerning the spirits. As he lay in bed for several months recovering from a leg injury, he spent time reading and thinking. He read the lives of the saints and imagined himself doing great things for God as did St. Francis and St. Dominic. Being a soldier, he also imagined himself being victorious in battle, receiving honors and seducing and courting beautiful women. Ignatius noticed that both of these fantasies gave him joy and delight. Upon reflection though, he noticed that the joy evoked from being a great warrior and lover was not lasting. The fantasies about doing great things for God, gave him a joy or consolation that was sustained over time. He noticed a difference in the quality of the joy. This experience laid the groundwork for his Exercises.

So we too are called to notice the quality of the consolations we experience. Consolations are those impulses to enjoy, grow, give and receive. God gifts you with attractions, tendencies, desires and power to help you move towards wholeness. It helps to go back to Jesus and the Gospel accounts. How did the Holy Spirit lead Jesus into a closer rela-

---

[16] *Ibid.*, #335, Rule 7 of the Second Week.

DISCERNING THE CALL

tionship with the Father? How did the Holy Spirit lead Jesus into an awareness of who he was called to be? How did Jesus know when he should move on to the next town? Begin his mission? Heal this person? When he should confront in anger like he did in overturning tables in the Temple?

I believe that Jesus was led by following those impulses that lead into deeper consolation. When Jesus marveled at the birds of the air or the flowers of the field, he grew in greater trust and faith in his Father's goodness. Those desires were a gift from the Spirit. When Jesus was grateful for creation, moved by the little children's trust and affection, enjoying a fishing trip and the quiet evening in the company of his friends, he grew in his love for God. Jesus was also led by the Spirit into the desert to be tempted. The Spirit can lead us into and through difficult places. The test is our growth in faith, hope and love.

Some examples of consolation might be the following:

- I may be fearful about a new ministry or responsibility in the parish. Suppose I am a lector for the liturgy. I am nervous wondering if I'll read well. Will I trip on my way to the lectern? Will I mispronounce the name of the Babylonian king? As I drive to the parish, the words from the Gospel come to me, "Fear is useless, only trust."

- For more than a year, the thought of becoming a priest or religious keeps bothering me. Finally, I get up the courage to ask my pastor for the phone number of the vocation office. I'm afraid I'll feel stupid asking him. What if he laughs? What if he discourages me from calling? When I do meet him, he expresses delight and encouragement and assures me of his support.

- Suppose I am angry and frustrated. I go to prayer and

49

put before God all my feelings. I list all I have to do today and the many things that cause me worry. I leave with a sense that God will take care of it all. I have a sense that God is in charge and have a deeper trust.

- While reading scripture, a certain word or phrase might jump out at me. I may have read this passage many times before, but today it speaks loud and clear. Although it challenges me, I feel peace at hearing the Word.

- It may be that I just taught a Confirmation class to high school students. I doubt that it made any difference to the teens. I wonder if I made myself understood or clear in my teaching efforts. On the way out, one of the students entrusts me with a problem. Something I said during the lesson touches this student.

- Perhaps I am experiencing a growing desire to read more, to learn more about God, to pray more. I want to be closer to God and not just know more about God.

You may experience consolation caused by something like a sunset, a memory of someone you love, or music. Consolations may also occur without a cause. Having been ruthlessly criticized and hurt, an "out of the blue" peace may come upon you as you realize that you are loved by God beyond anything you could ever imagine. This is consolation without cause.

When we live in consolation, our lives are in harmony. We live in faith, hope and love. We are able to perceive God's action in life. Consolation is a sense of well being.

Consolation is important because it gives us clear direction in the discernment process. Remember the significant moments of consolation in your life. Consolations are meant to be savored time and time again. God gifts us with

DISCERNING THE CALL

memory. When we relive experiences we have had of God, we can grow in faith, hope and love. Consolations give us the impetus to continue on the journey. They are manna for the hard times. Consolations are little revelations of God's love for you. They are reminders. God draws and courts you through these consolations. Just as our sufferings unite us with God, so do our consolations.

Desolation

We also experience desolation. The more we get to know ourselves and our vulnerabilities, the more easily we can halt spiritual desolation. A person can be led in to desolation by giving into ambition, pleasure, power, appearance, or human respect at the cost of his or her most authentic self. If we have a healthy prayer life, and are in touch with our feelings, we will be more aware of these movements. If not, we could be sucked into desolation and caught unaware. The tools that the evil spirit uses to draw us into desolation are fear, exaggeration, discouragement, self doubt, pride, and self pity. All of this works to distort who I really am.

I call desolation what is entirely the opposite of [consolation] what is described in the third rule, as darkness of soul, turmoil of spirit, inclination to what is low and earthly, restlessness arising from many disturbances who lead to lack of faith, lack of hope, lack of love. The soul is wholly slothful, tepid, sad and separated, as it were, from its Creator and Lord. For just as consolation is the opposite of desolation, so the thoughts that spring from consolation are the opposite of those that spring from desolation.[17]

_____
[17] St. Ignatius of Loyola, *Spiritual Exercises,* #317, 4th Rule of the First Week.

Desolation may be experienced within a group as well as by an individual. If you belong to a parish group or some other small community, you may have experienced this phenomenon. When jealousy, competition, possessiveness, desire to control, boredom, hatred, fear or pity is operative, the group is in desolation. Whenever manipulation is at work in a group, there is a movement of desolation. Reading the Gospels, Jesus never manipulates anyone into following him or into believing in him. Jesus always invites and leaves the person free to respond.

What would desolation look like for a person discerning a church vocation?

Here are some possible examples:

- I visit a religious community and they understand that I am in discernment. As the evening progresses, I feel uncomfortable with the innuendos that if I enter in the Fall, I would be part of a new program that would enable me to study in Europe. Pressure mounts through the evening as the group communicates that I am an answer to their prayers. They have been praying a special novena for a new candidate and that's me!

- A month after having been accepted into a brothers' community, I am offered a substantial promotion at work in a company. Since I have been on the corporate ladder for the last few years, I feel drawn to withdraw my application to become a brother. I am enticed by the money, power and prestige of the new position at work. Even though I have carefully discerned my call to become a brother over the last few years, I impulsively decide to go for the promotion.

- During the last year I have been discerning a call to diocesan priesthood. I have made retreats at the seminary, been in spiritual direction and am involved in my local parish. Over a few months' time, I have peacefully come to a decision to apply and have been accepted. Now thoughts of my unworthiness overwhelm me. I start worrying about my weaknesses. Even though I have been recommended by those who know me well, I experience darkness and doubts concerning my ability to really be a good priest.

- Having applied to the order of sisters to which I honestly feel God is calling me, I go through the application process. After the interviews, the vocation director informs me that there are some personal issues that I need to work on for another year before entering. She suggests that I go to counseling to work on these issues. I'm angry, and instead, find another community willing to take me two months from now.

St. Ignatius recommends some responses to our experience of desolation. These responses are for those whose lives are oriented towards God and those "in the state of grace." Otherwise, desolation is a reminder that the opposite is true. A person in serious sin, who experiences desolation, needs to listen to the darkness as a result of sin and an invitation to return to God!

When in desolation, recall a moment of consolation. Go back to an experience you have had of God. Relive the experience. Recall all of the details. Be specific about this experience of God in your life. Consolations are given to us for more than the moment. Consolations will carry us through the difficult times.

While in desolation, never make a major decision. This is not the time to make a decision. It is not the time to make any change in our plans, our spiritual life, or in our resolutions. To use a mundane example, if you have decided to walk three times a week for health and also to build in some reflection time, then don't stop when you get depressed or in some form of desolation. Walk through the desolation.

St. Ignatius also encourages us to go against the negative inclinations and do the opposite. For example, if you feel selfish, you could go out of your way to do something kind for another person; if you feel like complaining, try to compliment someone; if full of doubts, make an act of faith. St. Ignatius also suggests that in time of desolation, you intensify your prayer life and self reflection.

I love a comment that Thomas Merton made when asked about desolation. Someone asked him what he does when facing periods of dryness, boredom or restlessness in prayer. He said that he just holds on for the next supply! We know that there is a rhythm in the spiritual life. There are times of consolation, when we know we are loved and when we enjoy God's presence. There are other times when prayer is very difficult, when we don't "feel" God's presence and may even doubt God's existence. But we believe that we will experience consolation again so we hold on for the next supply!

Another word of warning: don't make hasty decisions and resolutions when you are caught up in the ecstasy of consolation. Take time to test the spirits. If you have a wonderful experience of God's presence, you may make a long list of dramatic and earth shattering changes in your life that you could never live up to in the real world.

Discerning the Spirits

St. Ignatius designed a meditation called "The Two Standards." He talks about the two directions and tugs that confront us – that of the Standard of Jesus and that of Satan. One key difference in the attraction is that Jesus invites us to something and Satan entices us. Those words are key in detecting which strategy is at work within us. Jesus *invites* because God respects our freedom. Jesus calls forth the best part of me. Satan *entices*, manipulates or seduces us through our compulsions, impulses and cultural pressures. Our freedom is compromised when we are hooked by enticements of money, power or prestige.

"Do not conform any longer to the pattern of this world, but be transformed by the renewing of your mind. Then you will be able to test and approve what God's will is – God's good, pleasing, and perfect will" (Romans 12: 2).

We do not have control over moods and feelings. Experiencing consolation and desolation is part of being alive. I don't plan my "bad hair days" anymore than I plan my surges of energy. The challenge is to go deeper. My identity in God is deeper than any of these movements. Discernment needs to go deeper to the initial impulse or affect and see where it originated. As we discern and pay attention to our thoughts and impulses we can decide to go with it, go against it, feed it or ignore it.

Noticing the affective movements in your life is crucial as you discern. A regular practice of "checking in" may help discernment of the spirits to become a natural, habitual way of remembering that your deepest choice is in God. When you're on the stationary bike at the gym, waiting for the bus, caught in traffic or standing in line somewhere, take note of where your heart rests; notice which of the dynamics are at work in you. Early recognition of a movement of desolation can enable you to counter it as you refocus on God and your deeper choice before the negativity can further drag you down.

In order to determine whether you are moving in consolation or desolation, trace the course of an experience. Look at the beginning, the middle and the end to see if there is a consistent direction to what is wholly good and entirely right. If at any point there is something evil, distracting or less good "than what the soul had formerly proposed to do," then carefully mistrust the experience. For example, you may decide you need more time for prayer. You begin well. After a few weeks, you find yourself competing with someone else's prayer life and spend longer and longer at prayer in order to appear "holier than thou." What began well went sour.

Similarly, if you start thinking about some personal weakness and begin berating yourself for that flaw, you might find yourself in a quicksand of despair. Considering our weaknesses outside the context of God's love and grace is a dangerous venture. A person could focus solely on weaknesses, feed negative thoughts and end up in serious desolation. What is important for your sanity and spiritual health is to recognize your tendencies right away and to know where you are vulnerable to being hooked into desolation. Act immediately with St. Ignatius' wisdom: remember a moment when you experienced God, don't make a decision, reflect, and go against the direction of the desolation, called "agere contra" with the opposite energy or virtue.

God's will for us is that we experience the fullness of life. Jesus said that he came to bring life and life to the fullest. The word "life" is mentioned 54 times in John's Gospel. God does not want us to wallow in self pity and beat ourselves up with negative thoughts. How can we minister to others, reach out to the needy, or create new possibilities for service, if we are chained up with an ugly sense of self?

DISCERNING THE CALL

Here, then, I have set before you life and prosperity, death and doom…I have set before you life and death, the blessing and the curse…Choose life then, that you and your descendents may live (Deuteronomy 30: 15 – 20).

Some Steps in the Process of Discerning

After spending time getting yourself to a place of openness and inner freedom, of plowing the soil of your heart, and believing the angel who says you're favored, you can begin a method of discerning. Throughout the process you need to pray for openness.

This eight-step process is only for major decisions. You don't want to discern trivial matters.

1. *Define* very clearly and succinctly *the matter for discernment*. Limit yourself to one focus statement. For example: "I will enter the seminary next Fall," or "I will enter a religious community next year."

2. *Gather relevant information*. This takes time.

    -   Read about priesthood or religious life.

    -   Participate in the Rite of Christian Initiation for Adults, or take some catechist formation classes if you need some basic Catholic spirituality and/or faith formation.

    -   Get information about the seminary, religious order, or diocesan priesthood from the diocesan vocation office. Attend vocation events like retreats, talks, or discernment groups. Browse through brochures, catalogues and vocation magazines.

3. *Use your imagination*. Do what St. Ignatius did. Spend time fantasizing. Imagine yourself as a priest or reli-

gious. Imagine yourself going through a typical day in your life 10 years from now if you were vowed or ordained. Notice how you respond on an affective level. Does it feel like it fits? You can do this fantasizing while shaving, driving, or waiting. At another time, imagine yourself as married or single. Imagine yourself continuing in your career or pursuing the career for which you were studying. Leave a space of time in between the fantasies.

4. Given your background, experience, gifts, talents, and weaknesses, is there any other possibility that you have not considered? You want to be open to all possibilities. Brainstorm! Create options you have never considered before. Imagination takes freedom.

5. Throughout the process, *pay attention to what God is saying.* What is God saying through the other people in my life, through the scriptures, through the events in my life? Keep a journal of those with significance for you and your future.

6. *Spend time listing* all the reasons against your decision (*the cons*). What would be the disadvantage of your becoming a sister, brother or priest? List these "cons." Spend a few days on the cons and continue the list. Notice what you experience internally as you consider them. Pray with them.

    Allow time to pass, few days or a week, then *list all of the advantages* for choosing a church vocation (*the pros*). What are the *pros* of making this choice? Write them down. Give yourself several days to ponder these pros and continue adding to the list.

    It does not matter how many cons or pros you list. You may have one pro and many cons and yet the weight of

DISCERNING THE CALL

the one advantage has more influence than many disadvantages. It is not a matter of numbers. This process will allow you to look at both sides of the issue in a prayerful context and enable you to grow in inner freedom.

7. Throughout the entire process, *keep checking in with your heart* to see what affective movements are stirring. Where do you experience peace? Real life? Hints of joy? Possibility? Energy? Hope?

8. *Go with the direction of consolation.* Talk over your pros and cons, your affective responses and what you learned from the information you gathered with a spiritual director. Come to a tentative decision through this consultation and prayer.

Confirmation

For a few weeks, or a suitable period of time, test the decision by living with it. Live as if you have definitely gone with your decision. Observe what you experience during this time. Confirmation comes with the experience of peace. If there are serious reservations and disturbance, then an alternative decision needs to be explored.

Part of the confirmation of your decision could be that things just fall into place. In some unexpected way you inherit money to help you pay off your student loans. You get accepted into the program of your choice. You receive encouragement and support from unexpected sources. Providence is obviously at work in your life. The excitement, joy and enthusiasm over a religious vocation may be further generated during the time of confirmation of the decision.

The opposite would be a sign to reconsider your decision. If you experience desolation, not just panic over the realities of entering, you need to bring the decision back to your spiritual director. A good decision should be accompanied by consolation. If the good decision is challenging, it may cost you in ways that cause some apprehension. But if you make a decision faithful to Gospel values, you should still experience peace at a deeper level.

If this peace endures over time, and there is a deeper sense that this is God's will, then you have confirmation. In personal discernment, sometimes this confirmation feels like a "coming home to self." It feels like you are your best self because of this particular choice.

An example of confirming joy and peace after a discernment, is described in the Acts of the Apostles, chapter 15. After a time of discernment, the apostles decided not to force the pagan converts to Christianity to follow Jewish customs. There was disharmony, tension, and confusion before the decision. After getting the word about the decision that was made, the Christian community experienced "great delight" – a sign of confirmation.

If the confirmation period affirms that your decision is spiritually healthy, then do not look back. There may be some initial panic or fear after the confirmation period when you realize what lies before you. I have noticed candidates for seminary or religious life discern carefully and well for a couple of years, and then after confirmation, they panic while packing their bags to enter. This is a normal reaction and not an indication that the discernment was poor.

As you grow in awareness of the different movements in your life, and of your struggles for inner freedom, you will develop kind of a "sixth sense" for discerning God's will. You will be more aware of the subtle nuances of God's action in your life. Compare it to an elderly married couple who know how to read one another's most subtle signs, gestures, facial expressions, and glances. As you develop a discerning heart, you will recognize the most gentle of invitation from God to love, to reach out, to respond. You will find yourself becoming more alert to the needs of others, detecting injustice, or perceiving risks to be taken. You will develop a sensitivity about who you really are and become aware of whether your life is in harmony with God. This awareness of harmony or dissonance will lead you in the choices you make.

Through the development of a discerning heart, you will be transformed into a prayerful person who can detect God's presence and action in a myriad of ways. Beyond "saying prayers," you may find that your life and very self become prayerful encounters with God.

St. Ignatius has a beautiful contemplation at the end of the Spiritual Exercises called, "The Contemplation to Attain Divine Love." The goal is to find God in all things. St. Ignatius reminds us that God labors in and through all of creation for our good. God dwells in the many gifts that grace our lives. The passion of our lives may become the facility and ability to find God in all things, rather than clinging to the security of past practices through which we may have been caught in a spiritual rut. This next section suggests ways to get out of the rut!

Using the Imagination

One of the most powerful gifts we possess is our imagination, yet as adults we enjoy this faculty too little. Children, though, know how to delight in possibilities and learn through imaginative exercises. A test of your inner freedom is the openness you have or don't, have to imaginatively entertain different possibilities.

Paul Ricouer said that imagination is integrally linked to our own *metanoia*, or conversion. "We too often and too quickly think of a will that *submits*, and not enough of an imagination that opens itself." Or, as Michael Himes paraphrases him, "Too often and too easily we tend to emphasize the need for conversion of the will when what is really required is an expansion of the imagination."[18] The founders of different religious communities had the inner freedom to imagine a new paradigm of ministry and religious life. Often it was one imaginative thought that provided the impetus for the birth of a religious order. The fruitfulness of one idea can extend from century to century. It was St. Ignatius' imagination that got him going.

A playful exercise while you are in discernment is to fantasize yourself founding a religious community. What experience of God have you had that would be incarnated in your vision of religious life? What would be the focus of your community? What kind of people would you look for? What rule of life would you consider, or would you not have one? What would bind the members together? This kind of fantasy will lend you clues as to your own sense of church, vocation and charism.

If you get "stuck" in discernment, grab a notebook, and write a letter to God very spontaneously. Don't worry about the spelling or what someone else might think if they read it. After reading over the letter, write God's response to you – again, very spontaneously. There is an inner wisdom to be tapped in us all.

Sometimes writing with the opposite of your preferred hand can give clues. No matter how awkward or ugly looking the writing, try to write something without thinking ahead what you are going to say. Ask your inner old wise

---

[18] Himes, Michael J. *Doing the Truth in Love*. New York: Paulist Press, p. 136.

DISCERNING THE CALL

person what advice she or he would give you. Write and see what surfaces.

Images can be a great help in discernment. Notice what particularly attracts you. Images could be icons, paintings, photos, a scene from a film, a memory. Collect images that speak to you. These could include newspaper or magazine cuttings. Pray with the images that come to you. St. Teresa of Avila used water in all its forms as a description for the development of a prayer life.[19] What images come to you? Some images may be culled from scripture, others from daily life.

What image leads you into stillness in prayer? Can you imagine yourself as a baby in the womb of God? Are you floating on your back in God's sea? Freely explore which images describe your present state.

Our images of God are only metaphors, as St. Thomas Aquinas tells us. We can never fully understand or name God, but each image can speak to us of God's different aspects. Which images of God are you most in tune with at this time of your life?

Get some crayons, markers, or pencils and by drawing freely, express your desires and hope, or some aspect of self.

Work with your dreams. Write down your dream in present tense. Bring it to prayer and listen to it. What are your common dream themes, characters or symbols?[20]

Imagine your future. Where would you like to be ten years from now? Twenty years from now? How old will you be? What would you like to be doing? What would you find most fulfilling and meaningful?

---

[19] Teresa of Avila, *Autobiography*.

[20] To further explore your dreams, consider using books such as Jeremy Taylor's *Dreamwork*. New York: Paulist Press, 1983; or Betsy Caprio and Thomas Hedberg's *At a Dream Workshop*. Paulist Press, 1987.

What does your inner child need? We all have memories growing up that have impacted our lives. You may have significant memories of yourself as a child of a certain age. It is good to revisit these memories as an adult in order to understand better who you are today. Think of a specific age at which you remember yourself as a child. Recall a critical incident that is engraved on your memory. It is good to "befriend" your child at this age by paying attention to her or his needs. It may mean doing something playful that you enjoyed at that age. Sometimes when an adult acts out, it is the inner child that they are not listening to or addressing. I believe that this inner child can remind us of what we might need, i.e., attention, affection, play. Part of discernment is growth in self-knowledge. It is possible that your inner child might give you some advice or insight. How? Here are some suggestions using you imagination and memory.

1. Imagine yourself at a certain age (6, 9, 11) and sit beside the little girl or boy you were at this age. Tell this child the story of your life so far. Tell the child who he or she will become when s/he grows up. This may give you a fresh perspective on your life.

2. What was your favorite activity at that age? Take your child out and do this activity.

3. At a quiet time, ask your child for advice concerning your discernment. What do you imagine your child is saying? If it helps, write a dialogue in the style of the script of a play, or of a conversation between you now and the child you used to be.

St. Ignatius suggests that imagining yourself on your deathbed can be a fruitful exercise. Consider which choice would you have wished you had made regarding your vocation as you lay dying. This meditation is meant to tap into

DISCERNING THE CALL

the wisdom that could be available to us at such an ultimate moment of truth.

Having focused on the imagination and its role in discernment, the next section examines religious life. Through imaginative vision, many holy women and men throughout history have brought to birth a variety of religious communities. Chapter four presents the development and diversity of religious life.

Confusion and the Search for Certainty

Uncertainty is not a "bad" place to be. Confusion reminds us that we are not God; that being in control is an illusion! The men and women of the scriptures spent a lot of time in confusion and doubt, lost in deserts, tempted, ridiculed and, at times, at odds with God. They knew that God can be found in darkness. "I know what it feels like to want God like I want my own breath. I know what it feels like to experience nothing but darkness and silence."[21]

Take the journey into and through the confusion. Don't sidestep the darkness. Go through the process and you will come out of it more in touch with yourself and more convinced of the faithfulness of God. "Darkness forces us inward…be open to the darkness that is present, listen to it, hear what it has to say, rather than trying to just survive with it or attempt to boot it out the door as quickly as possible."[22]

We all relive the pattern of the scriptures. If Jesus had to undergo the desert experience, why shouldn't we? We too get seduced by the fleshpots of Egypt; we wander around

[21] Wiederkehr, Macrina. *A Tree Full of Angels.* San Francisco: Harper and Row, 1988, p. 46.

[22] Rupp, OSM, Joyce. *Little Pieces of Light.* NY: Mahwah Illuniaion Books, Paulist Press. 1994, p. 15.

65

VOCATIONS ANONYMOUS

deserts for a long time. We get sidetracked with false gods at times. We meet God at unexpected graced moments that are forever etched in our memories. We think we know who God is and just as we get comfortable and settle into some sense that we know God, the Pentecost wind and flames come tearing through, shredding that certainty. The Spirit does this so that we'll move on to a deeper, truer image of God, leading us into the truth. Not easy…and not comfortable!

This is the experience of every baptized person on the faith journey (if they keep moving!), and not only the story of those in vocation discernment. Although, if you are being tossed and turned inside out with thoughts of priesthood and/or religious life, the experience may be intensified.

Some suggestions for dealing with this darkness:

1. Be honest about your lack of clarity. Admit that you do not have all the answers.

2. Gently sit with the uncertainty. Look your confusion "straight in the eye." Go to prayer and be your confused self before God. "Here I am, loving God, confused. Be with me in this place. Be light for me. Be peace for me."

3. Put your confusion in perspective. It is only one part of your entire life story. You have had other moments! St. Ignatius says that when you find yourself in darkness, you need to return to moments when you experienced God consoling you. What are the moments you need to return to and remember when God seemed close?

4. Write down your doubts and questions. Where are you confused? What confuses you?

DISCERNING THE CALL

And then...

- Go to a quiet place.
  Pray with a scripture verse. Here are a few suggestions: "If God is for us, who can be against us?" (Romans 8: 31); "For I am convinced that neither death, nor life, nor angels, nor principalities, nor present things, nor future things, nor powers, nor height, nor depth, nor any other creature will be able to separate us from the love of God in Christ Jesus our Lord" (Romans 8: 38, 39). This means that no confusion, uncertainty, darkness, etc. can separate us from the Love of Christ. You might choose to read the comforting last supper discourse from John 15.

- Listen.
  Ritualize your willingness to let go. One way of doing that is to take a paper on which you have written all your confusion and rip it to shreds.

WARNING: Don't jump to the last step before spending time with your own darkness.

Some suggested scripture to pray with when in confusion:

"For I know well the plans I have in mind for you…plans for your welfare, not for woe! Plans to give you a future full of hope." Jeremiah 29: 11

"You, Lord, are all I have and you give me all I need. My life is in your hands. How wonderful are your gifts." Psalm 16: 5,6

"Fear not, for I have redeemed you; I have called you by your name: You are mine. When you pass through the water, I will be with you…because you are precious in my eyes and I love you." Isaiah 43: 1,2

"By waiting and by calm you shall be saved, in quiet and in trust your strength lies." Isaiah 30:15

"This is what the Lord requires of you: to do justice, to love mercy and to walk humbly with your God." Micah 6:8

"Of you my heart speaks; you my glance seeks; your presence, O Lord, I seek." Psalm 27: 8

"Do not be afraid. I am with you…I will strengthen you and help you, and uphold you with my right hand of justice." Isaiah 41:10

"If you thirst, come to Me and drink. 'From within you there shall flow rivers of living water.'" John 7: 37,38

- *Habakkuk 2: 2–3*
- *Matthew 26: 36–46*
- *Romans 8*
- *Psalm 139*
- *Revelation 21: 1–7*
- *Luke 18: 35–43*
- *Psalm 23*
- *Matthew 27: 45–50*
- *Isaiah 43*
- *Jeremiah 29: 11–14*

Music for Prayer:

- "The Saint That Is Just Me" by Danielle Rose
- "Digo Si Señor" by Dona Peña
- "Small Things with Great Love" by Danielle Rose
- "Come Follow Me" by David Haas
- "Here I Am" Chris Silva
- "Go Make a Difference" Steve Angrisano
- Hermana Glenda's Music

DISCERNING THE CALL

- Servant Song

- "You Are Near"

- "Only in God" by Michael Talbot

Some artistic responses:

- Go to Prayer Windows http://www.prayerwindows.com for ideas on how to engage your creative self in the discernment process!

- Buy some inexpensive soft clay. Sculpt your confusion.

    - Change the shape as you move along your discernment process.

    - You will have a visual image for how you feel.

- Draw your confusion (It doesn't have to look like anything that anyone would recognize!)

- Draw a mandala of your discernment process or an image of your spiritual life.

- Sing out loud. Compose songs in the shower.

- Talk to someone who won't judge you, won't tell you what to do, who will not try to "solve your problems."

VOCATIONS ANONYMOUS

Here are some reflections by other Christians that may support your prayer:

My Lord God,
I have no idea where I am going.
I do not see the road ahead of me.
Nor do I really know myself,
And the fact that I think that I am following your will
Does not mean that I am actually doing so.
But I believe that the desire to please you
Does in fact please you.
And I hope that I will never do anything apart from
that desire.
And I know that if I do this,
You will lead me by the right road
Though I may know nothing about it.
Therefore will I trust you always though I may seem to
be lost
And in the shadow of death.
I will not fear, for you are ever with me,
And you will never leave me to face my struggles alone.

Thomas Merton[23]

---

[23] Merton, Thomas. *Contemplative Prayer.* Garden City, NY: Image Books, 1971.

God will enter into your night,
As the ray of the sun enters
Into the dark, hard earth
Driving right down
To the roots of the tree,
And there, unseen, unknown
Unfelt in the darkness,
Filling the tree of life,
A sap of fire
Will suddenly break out,
High above that darkness
Filling the tree with life
A sap of fire
Will suddenly break out,
High above the darkness,
Into living lead and flame.

Caryll Houslander

VOCATIONS ANONYMOUS

PART II
LIFESTYLES OF THE POOR, OBEDIENT AND CELIBATE

VOCATIONS ANONYMOUS

Chapter four
RELIGIOUS LIFE

Religious life has changed dramatically over the last fifty years since Vatican II which called us back to our original charisms and challenged us to read the signs of the times. We went through many changes in ministry, lifestyle, dress and prayer life after Vatican II. Some religious priests, sisters, and brothers left their orders in the 60's and 70's. The number of young adults entering religious life in the 50's and 60's was high. When many ministry opportunities as well as careers opened up for women, the numbers dropped. Catholics were very disturbed, and some still are, by the smaller number of people entering religious orders. You might hear comments like, "There aren't any sisters to teach in the schools anymore," or "The brothers gave us a great education in high school, where are they now?"

If we take a bird's eye view of the history of religious life, we will see the rise and fall of a variety of forms of religious life. In the third century, Anthony of the Desert drew men and women out to live a life of prayer, solitude and penance as hermits. In the 6th century, Benedict began a form of monastic life that drew thousands to community. During the Middle Ages, huge monasteries of men and women were centers of education, science, medicine and the arts. Thirteenth century mendicant orders were founded by visionaries like St. Francis of Assisi and St. Dominic Guzman who inspired women and men to live a new form of religious life. The mendicants were dependent on alms for support. This freed them to pray and bring the gospel message to people in the newly emerging towns.

In the 16th century, the Reformation ushered in another new form of religious life. The Society of Jesus (Jesuits) was founded by St. Ignatius of Loyola in 1540. The Jesuits were committed to go anywhere to serve the needs of the Church. New religious communities of women also responded to new needs. Sisters moved out of the cloister to serve the poor. The Ursulines in 1535 and the Sisters of Charity in 1614 dedicated themselves to care for the needs of the poor. John Baptist de la Salle founded an order of brothers who educated youth. New orders of missionaries grew during the 16th and 17th centuries as explorers ventured into new lands.

Each religious order has a charism, a specific gift that defines its mission and spirituality. The charism empowered the founders to respond with a distinctive service to the Church, a specific ministry or spirituality. Charism is the way a particular order incarnates the Gospel message. Some religious orders died out when their charism was no longer needed in the Church, for instance, those orders that were ministering to slaves on ships.

Many of the various forms of religious life which have developed throughout history continue today. Some people are called to be hermits. There is a Camaldolese monastery in Big Sur, California. Hermits are fewer these days, but still a recognized vocation with people willing to respond. Communities of contemplative women and men are flourishing around the country. Even though there are fewer people in monasteries than during the Middle Ages, the

Trappists and Trappistines, Cistercians, Benedictines, and Poor Clares among others are contemplative communities still attracting women and men to their prayerful way of life.

There are many active apostolic religious throughout the world. Women and men, priests, brothers and sisters, organized around the charisms of their founders, continue a diversity of ministries with a common spirituality and mission. They serve as pastors of parishes, lawyers in defense of the poor, psychiatrists, teachers, pastoral ministers, artists, community organizers, health care workers, and in any ministry where they can proclaim the goodness of God with their lives.

If you charted the different forms of religious life according to membership numbers throughout history, you would observe a rise and fall rhythm.

Each form of religious life continues today: hermits, monks, cloistered nuns, mendicants, monastics, active apostolic religious, missionaries and others, sometimes in fewer numbers than in the past.

Perhaps we are on the verge of a new development. Many religious orders are finding new life in their associate membership. Often these associates are invited to the meetings, called chapters, which communities have to plan their future. For example, in the 1970's, the Immaculate Heart Community "widened the space of their tent," so to speak, to include other vocations. Single and married, and non-vowed members join the IHM's for days of prayer, ministry, workshops and ministry. Usually associates are alumni of the IHM's schools, former vowed members, or people captivated by the spirit of the congregation who want to identify more closely with it.

From the historical perspective, we have seen three major cultural shifts in the Western world during the last 500 years: the Reformation, the French Revolution, and the present time. Both the Reformation and the French Revolution were characterized by a decrease in priests and religious, and then followed by a new surge of membership in religious communities.

What about our current situation? Where is it all going? Some communities feel called to preserve the traditions of their lives together, while others feel moved to explore a new paradigm of religious life. Most religious are not sure about what religious life will look like in the future. In the face of uncertainty, there is a lot of trust, creative planning, and stumbling to be done between now and "then." But the essentials of religious life are likely to remain. In addition to the vows, there are three other elements that characterize the call to religious life. Ideally, religious are supported by a community, nourished by a communal and personal prayer life, and energized by ministry.

Most religious take three vows: poverty, chastity and obedience. Some religious take a fourth vow; for example, to serve the poor, or to remain in a certain monastery for life. The way the vows are lived changes throughout history.[24]

One example from my own life is that of how the vow of obedience has changed. After I was professed, I was told that I would be going to St. Hedwig's Catholic School to teach the second grade. I moved the next day. I did not have a credential or college degree at that time, and needless to say, I had never taught full time. I simply packed up and moved. That was in 1970.

By contrast, in 1986, when I returned from Africa, my

---

[24] See Chapter 5, Vows.

superior told me to take time to readjust to life in the States. She suggested that I peacefully and gently explore any possible ministries opening up. I prayed and looked around. It was limbo time for me. Life had changed a lot in the States during the seven years I had been away. Shortly after I returned, I gave a vocation talk, and was invited to apply for the vocation director position in the Los Angeles Archdiocese. The idea appealed to me, so I checked it out with my superior, and she encouraged me to go for it. Then I discovered that I was to send in my resume and present myself for interviews. I never thought that as a sister I would have to write a resume. Without the slightest idea of how to begin, I relied on the local library for help with crafting my resume. This experience was a long way from my earliest years in community when I was told what to do without being consulted. Religious life had changed, and the only way to survive was to adapt! This model challenged me to be more responsible and discerning, and included me in the process of ministry agreement.

Another example is in the financial and educational responsibilities of those in religious life. In 1950, Rome told communities of women religious that their members should seek employment that wouldn't distract them from prayer, as they would no longer be supported by donations. Since that time, the educational level of women religious has increased dramatically. A 1989 study showed that 83% of all sisters had at least a BA; 62% of all sisters had their Masters or PhD. The numbers are even higher now. I read somewhere that the most highly educated sector of the American population are women religious.

For me, living as a religious in this day and age is exciting. I am challenged to discover new ways of being faithful, of living Gospel values, of belonging to a community. Creatively struggling to live out a new vision of community and ministry as a religious stretches me, rather than allowing me to stagnate in old securities. Most religious brothers and priests that I work with experience similar hope for the future, even though often it is unclear just where we are headed.

Research has shown that religious communities follow a predictable cycle of growth from founding to maturity.[25] As you begin to explore different orders, understanding this cycle might be helpful. During the first 10 to 20 years, the *founding years*, the founder relies on the kernel of the conversion experience and begins to live it out in some form of community and ministry.

The *expansion period* follows, fired up by the enthusiasm of new beginnings and numerical growth. Community norms and policies are established at this time. For the next 50 to 100 years, the members of the order set about their apostolate with success and purpose. This is called the *stabilization period*. During the next fifty years, the *breakdown period*, disillusionment may set in, and there can be a loss of identity and polarization.

The *critical period* presents the religious order with three options: extinction, minimal survival or revitalization. Revitalization is like a re-founding of the order and also calls for personal conversion. Extinction is not peculiar to our time. 76% of all religious orders founded before 1500 no longer exist. Some religious communities existed at a point in time for a specific purpose and then died out.

Whereas the diocesan priesthood involves service within a specific diocese in union with the local bishop for the people of that diocese, religious life enables women and

---

[25] "The Life Cycle of a Religious Community," *Shaping the Future of Religious Life.*

men to serve where they are most needed, often beyond the geographical boundaries of their motherhouse or congregation center. For this reason, religious throughout history have been known to be inventive about meeting contemporary needs and making ongoing adjustments.

The diminishing number of religious does not have to be bad news. Within historical and developmental perspective, it is natural and predictable. It is the Paschal mystery being lived in community: dying and rising, achieving and letting go. Many religious who formally owned huge generalates and community houses have left them to live in much simpler environments and in poorer neighborhoods. This speaks of the transformation in the effort to live Gospel values.

The Future of Religious Life

What might life as a brother, sister or religious priest look like in the future? In 1989, two professional organizations of women and men religious offered their description of the transformative elements for religious life in the year 2010.[26] They focused on ten elements. The following is a summary of their work.

1. *Prophetic Witness:* Religious will have a prophetic role in challenging society and the Church to be faithful to the Gospel. Living this prophetic witness will include critiquing societal and ecclesial values and structures, calling for systematic change and being converted by the marginalized with whom we serve. Dramatic evidence of this role is seen in the case of the women martyred in El Salvador in 1980 while helping to educate and liber-

---

[26] Transformative Elements for Religious Life. Conference of Women Religious and Conference of Major Superiors of Men, 1989.

ate the Salvadoran people.[27]

2. *Contemplative Attitude Toward Life:* Religious communities in 2010 will be centers of contemplation and spirituality for the whole Church. They will be attentive to and motivated by the presence of the sacred in their own journeys, in the lives of others, and through creation. Already many religious invite people to pray with the community and to share life.

3. *Poor and Marginalized Persons as the Focus for Ministry:* The focus of religious will be to minister where no one else will go. For example, religious women and men were among the first to engage in AIDS/HIV ministry. Oftentimes religious creatively find new ways of being present to the poor and enabling people to develop and grow in some independence, in spite of not having financial resources. More recently, women religious have been fighting to abolish human trafficking, a modern form of slavery.

4. *Spirituality of Wholeness and Global Connectedness:* As we discover more about the cosmos, its beginnings and its subatomic nature, we realize just how interdependent we are with the earth and with each other. What happens in a South American rainforest affects life in North America and around the globe. Religious hope to lead the way through a spirituality that would acknowledge this global interconnectedness, and through ministry, try to build community among all peoples.

5. *Charism and Mission as Sources of Identity:* Often the revitalization of religious communities involves a return to the original charism and mission of the order. Some religious communities who share common charisms

---

[27] The Jesuits' Salvadoran housekeeper and her daughter were also murdered.

RELIGIOUS LIFE

and vision are joining together. Communities will continue to grow towards a more focused mission and clearer "corporate" identity.

6. *Change of the Locus of Power:* Religious communities are moving towards a collaborative model of power-sharing and decision-making and away from hierarchical structures. Models of domination and control will be replaced with principles of mutuality drawn from feminist and ecological insights.

7. *Living with Less:* Religious hope to live with less and grow in reverence for the earth. Consumerism and many of its wasteful and toxic by-products are destroying creation. Religious hope to be witnesses of a joy that comes from having less.

8. *Broad-based, Inclusive Communities:* Many communities have already made efforts to include members of different ages, genders, cultures, races and sexual orientations to mirror the reality of the Body of Christ. Broad based, inclusive communities may well characterize the active apostolic religious life of the future.

9. *Understanding Ourselves as Church:* Religious hope to work towards shared leadership and respect for the quality of all members. What would distinguish religious life from other forms of Christian life "is the fact that religious life raises to explicit articulation in lifestyle that which is common to all Christians, namely, the vocation to follow Jesus by leaving behind all that impedes our discipleship so that we can freely participate in his filial identity and his salvific mission."[28]

_____

[28] Lozano, John. *Discipleship: Towards and Understanding of Religious Life.* Chicago: Claret Center for Resources in Spirituality, 1980.

83

10. *Developing Interdependence Among People of Diverse Cultures:* With the growth in the cultural diversity of our population, religious will also strive to uncover the racism, prejudices, and intolerance that stand in the way of developing the interdependence of cultures.

Why Consider Religious Life?

Why would anyone desire to become an active apostolic religious sister or brother today? I propose some good reasons for considering religious life:

- To identify for life with a group of people who share a common gospel vision and common values. (I meet many young adults who want to share life with people of similar beliefs and values. Belonging to a parish group or basic Christian community does not seem to be enough.)

- To be rooted in a historically grounded community with the mobility and freedom to respond to the signs of the times and the needs of God's people. There is a value to belonging to a group that has a sacred history. Religious life also affords us the freedom and mobility to move out into new ministries.

- To live on the cutting edge; to promote justice in the world and the Church. Religious usually continue attending workshops, reading and engage in ongoing formation to keep on their toes.

- To enjoy the opportunity to work alongside a variety of people, loving them freely, regardless of race, gender, age, health or culture. (This is the heart of the commitment to be a celibate lover, to love inclusively.)

RELIGIOUS LIFE

- To accept the challenge and the invitation to help forge the future development of religious life for the 21st century.

- To serve God's people in a variety of ministries using your talents and gifts and being supported by community.

One thing we can be certain about in religious life: it is a life of change. In 1995, I took a course at Notre Dame University called, "God and the New Physics," taught by Fr. Kevin O'Shea. What physicists are discovering today will change our world view. This will impact philosophy, theology, and spirituality. When Galileo discovered that the sun did not revolve around the earth, it changed forever the way people understood their place in the universe. Subsequently, it affected all the other disciplines. In a video on religious life, Sr. Amata Miller, IHM, says "the rest of our lives must be spent in the best of struggles."[29] Are you called to invest your energy to help envision a religious life for the future? The current reality and the uncertainty of the future are both part of the discernment process.[30]

Community

Women and men religious are called to community life. Sometimes they live alone and have to intentionally make connections to make community a reality. Ideally, community offers support of living the vowed life and ministry. My best community experiences have been places in which I could be myself and share the joys and struggles of the sis-

[29] Miller, IHM, Amata, *Religious Life: The Constant is Change. A Video Presentation on Religious Life in the Post-modern era.* Monroe, MI.

[30] For further reading consult David Nygren, CM, and Miriam Ukeritis, CSJ, *Future of Religious Orders in the United States: Transformation and commitment.* Westport, Conn.: Praeger, 1994.

85

ters with whom I lived. Sharing faith in community enables religious to share what God is doing in their lives with people of like minds. Belonging to a community gives a religious the impetus to reach out to others in ministry.

Preparation for community life requires an ability to give and take, to be flexible, and to adjust to different temperaments, cultures, and situations. Most religious communities are made up of people who would not choose to live together under different circumstances. This calls for an effort to build a community of faith and trust. In preparation, they try to be on the alert for others' needs, ready to contribute, rather than to fulfill ones' own need for friendships.

Most communities have adapted community life to changing ministries and varying timetables. Prayer together takes on different shapes and forms, given the order. Some active communities meet weekly for a "sharing of the heart" or reflection on a scripture passage. Others meet several times each day to pray the Liturgy of the Hours and Eucharist.

Brothers

An often misunderstood vocation is that of the *brother*. Because of their relatively large numbers, sisters have been much more visible. The sacramental ministry of priests places them regularly in the public eye. But brothers have often been left out of the vocation scene. They often teach in classrooms and work in hospital settings like women religious do. They are frequently behind the scenes and perform a wide range of ministries that contribute to the Church. There aren't as many brothers as sisters in the Church, but theirs is a vital and life-giving ministry.[31]

[31] For more information about religious brothers, consult Michael F. Meister, FSC, ed., *Blessed Ambiguity. Christian Brothers Conference.* Winona, MN: St. Mary's Press, 1993.

RELIGIOUS LIFE

In case you have never met or known a religious brother, you might wonder about his particular vocation. What is a brother? A brother is a vowed member of a religious order who ministers through a particular profession or trade. Brothers are not ordained. There are two types of religious orders for brothers. Some communities are composed solely of brothers, like the Christian Brothers de La Salle, the Irish Christian Brothers, or the Brothers of the Sacred Heart. Other religious orders will accept men who wish to be brothers or priests, as do the Jesuits, the Franciscans and the Benedictines.

Religious brothers are involved in a wide variety of ministries in ways similar to women religious. Just as there are differing lifestyles among sisters of religious communities, so too, the communities of brothers are just as varied in mission, focus and lifestyle. Since the religious life includes all those in religious orders, all that has been said above applies to brothers. What is the special gift of brothers to the Church? Here is the perspective of one brother:

> The ability of brothers to bond with all peoples, the solidarity and fraternity they have nourished in their ranks, the purification they have experienced in the fires of change, their dream of participating in the refashioning of a broken world into a global family where justice and compassion reign, instead of oppression and racism – here may be found the seeds of brotherhood for tomorrow. The task may seem formidable, quixotic, beyond reach. But like a candle burning at the edge of dawn, let us dream, and let the dream intoxicate us into believing that it is possible.[32]

One fundamental commitment that all brothers, sisters and religious priests share in common is the vows. Chapter 5 provides an overview of the vowed life.

---

[32] *Ibid.* p. 238

VOCATIONS ANONYMOUS

Chapter five

VOWS

The Church does not take vows lightly. A vow is a sacred promise or commitment made publically with the approval of the Church. It usually takes several years of candidacy, novitiate and temporary promises before one makes final vows in a community. The Church requires a canonical examination of the candidate before final profession to ensure that the person is genuinely free and not unduly influenced or coerced into such a commitment.

Most religious take three vows: poverty, chastity, and obedience. Some communities presently name the vows: simplicity of life, celibacy, and obedience. Some monastic communities take a fourth vow of *stability*. The monastery they enter remains their home for life, unless they are called to be part of a new foundation. Some exceptions are made for study, illness or family need. Other communities take a fourth vow to serve the poor or some other commitment associated with their charism.

The vows are meant to free those who profess them for service and common life, with freedom to be mobile in ministry. The understanding of the vows has evolved many times during the last fifty years as religious struggled to redefine them so that they continue to reflect Gospel values given the signs of our times. "This transformation is a function both of cultural evolution and of the theological awakening of the twentieth century. The understanding and practice of the vows is moving away from an emphasis on the assumption obligations and toward an emphasis on commitment to personal spiritual growth and to participation in the world-transforming mission of the Church."[33]

The vows are a witness to God's reign and counter-cultural statement to both the world and the Church. Religious life reminds the Church and the world of the prophetic, ecclesial and eschatological dimensions of God's reign. Some religious orders were founded as a critical response to the way society treated certain people. Through their *fuga mundi*, or flight from the world, monks challenged the growing worldliness of the clergy. The Carmelites stood out in sharp contrast to the Church and to the geopolitical realities of the Spain of the fourteenth and fifteenth centuries. When the Sisters of Adoration dedicated their time and energy to ministry with prostitutes, they were protesting the condition of women in the nineteenth century.[34]

The evolution of the vow of poverty today calls religious to be prophetic in the "human effort to convert the race from exploitation to responsible stewardship, to liberate the poor by an equitable distribution of goods, to create the economic structures which will effectively relate finite resources to human ends."[35]

Living the vows was formerly very clear because the rules were laid down very clearly and definitively. For example, we were not allowed to keep private possessions or to touch another sister (we gave a little tug on the veil!). We also asked permission for very specific daily activities. That strict observance began to change with the realization that

---

[33] Schneiders, Sandra. *New Wineskins, Towards a Contemporary Theology of the Vows.* New York: Paulist Press, 1986, pp. 93 – 94.

[34] Lozano, CMF, John. "In the Service of the Reign of God," p. 63.

[35] *Ibid.*, Schneiders, p. 103.

a vow is much more than adherence to rules. It is a way of living life. It is a disposition that orients my choices. Sr. Barbara Fiand, SND, writes, "I vow a movement into God. I vow to allow myself to be changed. I submit and surrender to that change."[36] She describes the vows as a journey into depth that is a lifelong process.

The challenge for me has been to keep reflecting on what being faithful means. As circumstances change – the environment, community life, or our understanding of being religious – they effect change in the way the vows are lived. Religious life is one organic whole comprised of community, prayer, ministry and the vows. As the understanding of one aspect develops, all the other aspects are affected as well.

Let me try to paraphrase what each vow might mean for a religious today.

Obedience comes from the Latin word, *obedire*, which means "to listen." There is a communal aspect to the vow of obedience. We are called to listen as a community to the Word of God, to the signs of the times in events and society, and to the Church to see *where* we are being called and *what* we are being called to do. On the personal level, the vow of obedience requires a prayer life that cultivates a listening heart. The Gospel image that I keep before me for this vow is imagining Jesus listening to God and responding as he did in the desert, in the garden, on top of a mountain, or through someone like the Syro-Phoenician woman. Jesus was obedient because he listened and responded to what he heard.

When I took a vow of obedience, I did not give up my intelligence, my responsibility, my preferences, or my personality. Being obedient, for me, means a call to really listen

[36] Fiand, SND, Barbara. *Living the Vows in an Age of Change.* NY: Crossroad. 1990.

to my deepest stirrings, to my sisters in community and to God, and not just to do what I want to do! It calls me to a poverty of spirit and an emptiness, rather than an attitude of having all the answers.

The challenge comes with hearing something that may seem impossible. In religious life, I've done things I'd never dreamt I would ever be able to do. All is gift and was done through God's grace, but it does require an initial "yes." With every risk I've taken beginning a new ministry, I've experienced all the gifts I needed for that particular ministry. From classroom teaching to giving retreats, teaching swimming to running a marathon, giving a piano recital or interviewing men for the seminary, I experienced God actualizing the potential within me to respond.

If you want to prepare for religious life, continue working on the ability to trust, to let go and to surrender. Obedience challenges us to be flexible and adaptable. If you have had authority issues because of your parents or your personal history, and have a need to control, you may experience this dimension of religious life as very difficult.

Poverty, or *simplicity of life*, is a commitment to sharing, not only of possessions, but of your time, talents, and presence. Poverty challenges religious to live simply in joyful dependence of God, standing in solidarity with the poor and challenging the structures that oppress.

In some communities, the expression of poverty is contingent on the ministry at hand. When I was living in the bush in Zambia, a bucket and a flashlight were two of my most prized possessions! With all the traveling I do now to attend meetings and give retreats, my laptop computer enables me to get work done on the plane. In Zambia, I waited for a bus once for three days. In Los Angeles, I have the sole use of a car for ministry. Yet sometimes I experience poverty as I stand before a group to speak, with butterflies in my stomach!

The vow of poverty has taught me to trust in Divine Providence. Poverty has taught me that all is gift. As Barbara Fiand writes, poverty is a movement into God as opposed to a movement to ego enhancement; "poverty is not something we do or practice, but something we are." An authentic living of the vow frees us to share generously and not be penny pinchers! It gives us the ability to do without cheerfully and with purpose.

If you are preparing to live the vow of poverty, try now not to buy into the all pervasive consumer mentality. This means much more than not possessing things. Poverty means an openness to share all I am and have. It may mean giving my time when I'd rather do something else, or pitching in for a community celebration by offering a talent I have – cooking, music, decorating or organizing.

All Christians are called to be chaste. Not all Christians are called to be celibate. That is why today most religious talk about the vow of *celibacy*. Celibacy is the promise to love wholeheartedly and inclusively all God's people. Celibacy calls me to be a warm, loving and vibrant person. There is a joke that will make this point. A senior sister who was very stern said, "I'm going to heaven with my vow of chastity intact! I have never loved anyone!" That is *not* the idea! Celibacy challenges us to be free of married commitments and from other relationships so that we are open and ready to love especially the unlovable. I am called not to limit my love to one person, husband or one family, but to make myself available for the Gospel, free to go anywhere, ready to love any person. Celibacy calls me to pledge my love to Jesus *totally* in order to love other people.

For me, celibacy has been a life-giving experience. Although I have had my struggles with different aspects of celibacy during different times, I have had a life rich in relationships, intimacy, and generativity. What I have experienced as a religious outweighs any loss I have felt with regard to not having my own child.[37]

The next chapter offers some suggestions for persons in discernment on living this counter-cultural vow. It addresses the special issues and concerns of living celibacy in modern society.

---

[37] See Chapter 13: The Baby Issue.

Chapter six

SEXUALLY ALIVE AND CELIBATE

Skills for Celibate Lovers

- ✓ A strong prayer life (the willingness to spend quality time with God; the openness to grow in intimacy with God)

- ✓ Long term friendships with both men and women

- ✓ The ability to be alone (to use solitude creatively and constructively)

- ✓ The gift to love tenderly and walk humbly with others

- ✓ Ability to delay gratification

- ✓ The freedom not be to self-absorbed, but to reach out to others

- ✓ A wholesome balance and integration of social, physical, intellectual and spiritual resources

- ✓ Ego boundaries – a sense of self; identity

Do you realize that everything you do is sexual? The way you walk, talk, pray, create, and relate are all ways of being in this world as a sexual person. A healthy, celibate person is very much aware of how sexuality pervades everything he or she does. Sexuality lives in one's body, one's mind, emotions, spirituality, and personality. Sexuality is an awareness of one's gender. It is much more than sexual activity. Celibates are called to be sexual persons and to live lives without interpersonal genital sexual activity. Each baptized person, whether married or single, priest or religious, is called to live a chaste life. The vow of celibacy is one way of loving as a sexual person.

Sexuality and spirituality are closely connected. St. Teresa of Avila was a passionate woman. Her descriptions of mystical prayer are in many ways very sexual. For example, she wrote about being on fire within:

> Now, it often happens, when the soul, continuing her way, all on fire within, has a passing thought, or hears some word suggesting that death is long in coming, that she seems to receive a blow, coming from elsewhere, she knows not whence nor how, but it is as if she were struck by a fiery dart…it inflicts a severe wound, and not, in my opinion, in that part where, naturally speaking, we feel pain, but in the most profound and intimate depths of the soul, where this bolt of fire, which descends so swiftly, reduces to powder whatever it finds of our earthly nature.[38]

It seems that spirituality and sexuality can be reconciled within oneself in such a way that one fuels the other in an effort to be more loving and united with God. Another person who could see this relationship was Carl Jung. He wrote:

But in mysticism, one must remember that no "symbol-

---

[38] Teresa of Jesus. *The Interior Castle.* Westminster, Maryland: The Newman Bookshop, p. 100.

ic" object has only one meaning; it is always several things at once. Sexuality does not exclude spirituality, nor spirituality sexuality, for in God all opposites are abolished.[39]

Celibates experience both sexual and spiritual passion. The challenge is to welcome and integrate sexuality by paying attention. Becoming more "spiritual" means an integration and transformation of all aspects of my being, including my sexuality. Being holy does not mean that I deny, repress, or ignore my sexuality. It means I give thanks and praise that I am a sexual person.

The Incarnation is at the heart of our Christian faith. We believe that the Incarnation means that God became flesh, a human being complete and full. How was Jesus sexual and celibate? Usually people do not want to think of Jesus as sexual, as though it might be irreverent. If the whole point was to become flesh, don't you think that God would want us to listen to that reality?

Jesus broke the rules regarding sexual taboos. Jesus talked to women who were strangers. He kept company with prostitutes. Jesus allowed a bleeding woman to touch him. Jesus traveled with women. Jesus healed women by touching them. Jesus moved beyond the cultural taboos and religious laws to speak to women, to be touched by them and to love them. Mary sat at the feet of Jesus; this was indicative of a disciple relationship. Jesus taught Mary in the tradition of the Jewish faith. Women were not to be taught in this capacity. Jesus wept when his friend Lazarus died. He went to his friends' house just to relax. Is this the Jesus who you know?

If Jesus were interviewed today and asked how to live celibacy well, would he say, "Be careful, keep your affection

---

[39] Jung, Carl. *The Collected Words of C.G. Jung.* Volume 14, Sir Herbert Read, Michael Fordham, Gerhard Adler, eds. NY: Bollingen Foundation, 1963. #634.

to yourself, or don't be seen alone with someone of the same or opposite sex or of ill repute?" NOT! Jesus would probably say, "My friendships supported me; going out to others in love gives meaning to my life. The time I spent in prayer early in the morning, in a garden, on a hill or in the desert, saw me through because I was always united with God."

Our culture is sexually obsessed. This stuck me all the more when I lived in Africa without any of the pervasive media, magazines, or newspapers that are so filled with sexual stimuli. The point was brought home at a time when we had trouble getting water.

The pump at the river broke down and the parts were not available for two weeks. It was not safe to go into the river because of snakes, crocodiles, and disease. We had just enough water to drink, but none for washing. One day, some of the African sisters and I walked through the deep sand to the river with buckets. We decided to try to strain some of the water through a filter and attempt to wash ourselves. On the way to the riverside, I received a letter from home and began to read it. The letter was from some of my sibling sisters back home who were worried about me. They had had a discussion at home about my life and decided that without a sex life, I couldn't really be happy and whole. Here I was, in 110° heat, and my siblings were worried about how I would gratify my sexual drive! At the time, all I wanted was water!!!

Even though in our culture it seems that people are preoccupied with sexual expressions, what they really hunger for is intimacy. We hunger for it and are frightened by it. Culturally we have seen how people can be naked and not reveal who they are. People can give over their bodies and withhold their real selves. Most people who are in addictive patterns of gambling, sex, food, alcohol, or drugs are really

SEXUALLY ALIVE AND CELIBATE

longing for intimacy. Intimacy means the capacity for emotional, physical and spiritual connectedness with another person. Intimacy is the capacity to be truly yourself with another person as well as to create a trust in which the other person can reveal the self as well.

The best celibates I know are warm, energetic, alive, loving people. They are not dried up, cold sterile men and women. If you were asked to name a priest, sister or brother whom you admired during your teen or young adult years, who would that person be? What one-word adjective would you use to describe that person? List them. Read the list. Does it sound like a description of a celibate person to you? Most often, the list contains words like: fun, loving, caring, faith-filled, compassionate, prayerful, wise, encouraging, affirming, and selfless.

The purpose and meaning of celibacy is to create better lovers! The idea is that we are moved to reach out in love to other people, especially the "unlovable" in society. Celibacy frees us to love old, sick, forgotten, imprisoned, dying and neglected people. If we shun these people, we are not loving inclusively, which is the purpose of celibacy. A celibate person who guards the self in order to "preserve" a vow, and protects the self with a comfortable lifestyle, is narcissistically living a travesty of celibate commitment.

Fr. Bill Jarema, author of *Fathering the Next Generation: Men mentoring Men*[40], refers to the four things that make good sex which also make good celibacy. Good sex is always procreative; good celibacy creates life wherever a celibate goes! Good sex is re-creative and fun; celibacy is rich in relationships. Good sex is transformative; celibacy is transforming. It pulls us out of ourselves. Good sex is social;

---

[40] Jarema, William J. *Fathering the Next Generation: Men Mentoring Men.* NY: Crossroad. 1994.

celibacy draws one out of self into relationships of service, friendship, and family.

The most dangerous thing about celibacy is not struggling with abstinence from genital sex; it is the danger of becoming selfish! Celibates usually don't have to get up a 2 a.m. to feed a baby, or have to change their plans because of a spouse or the kids. Celibates take care of themselves and those they serve. The danger of celibacy is that it can turn a person inward instead of outward. The booby trap of celibacy is to be trapped in self absorption.

When I was in the novitiate, I thought that chastity was something I had and needed to protect. A wise priest later on taught me that celibacy was something I would struggle for and hopefully win in the end! Celibacy is a process of falling in love and growing into a lover. They say that the average adult falls in love seven times in their lifetime. This doesn't mean that the adult has to run off and have an affair. We will inevitably find attractive people that we are drawn to during our lifetime.

Celibates experience intimacy in trusting relationships and also through ministry. Some people trust priests and religious with the secrets of their lives. Even on a plane, I am always shocked by the amount of self disclosure that people risk with me as a stranger when they discover that I am a sister – after their second Bloody Mary! Celibates experience intimacy in prayer, in the myriad of caring signs from God in daily life, in the car, at the beach, the gym and all those places non-celibates experience intimacy with God.

What helps us to live celibacy well? Being honest with God in prayer and with a spiritual director or confessor is absolutely, totally necessary. In my own struggles, I have found that going to prayer without being honest is a waste of time. Bring it all into the Light. Expressing my deepest longings and hungers to God has given my celibate commitment meaning because it is relational. My best friends have helped me to grow towards authentic celibacy. Having a good support group of friends and family enables celibates to live fruitfully. Paying attention to the body is crucial for celibates. If I live outside of my own body by ignoring my physical needs, then disaster is just around the corner. Exercising, good nutrition, rest, touching and being touched appropriately are healthy ways to maintain an awareness of the physical self.

There are stages in a celibate's life when different issues come to the fore. During early adulthood, sexual tension and the longing for one companion can be challenging. Later on the desire to have a child kicks in with the biological clock ticking and the realization that having a child will never happen. Midlife brings its own challenges with the need to reflect on life's meaning, regroup, recommit and move from the emphasis of *doing* to *being*. Carl Jung writes that we can't live the afternoon of life with the morning's program. In midlife we are not driven by the same desire to achieve, prove ourselves and make our mark. Celibates also deal with meaning and wrestle with how their lives are generative. If there are no offspring, where has life been sown? Celibates also generate life and leave something to grow.

God seduced me into celibacy. When I was eighteen, I was madly in love with God. In prayer I experienced a delightful intimacy with God. I could feel God's presence. I knew I was loved by God and felt a burning passion to love God in return. I entered the convent young and really confronted the celibacy issues later on after God already had me hooked. This is not an unfamiliar pattern from what I understand! There is a sonnet by John Donne, a bold prayer that reflects how the experience of God's love can woo us into lives of chaste love.

> *Batter my heart, three-personed God; for You*
> *As yet but knock, breathe, shine, and seek to mend;*
> *That I may rise and stand, o'erthrow me, and bend*
> *Your force to break, blow, burn and make me new.*
> *I, like an usurped town, to another due,*
> *Labour to admit You, but O, to no end;*
> *Reason, Your viceroy in me, me should defend,*
> *But is captive, and proves weak or untrue,*
> *Yet dearly I love You, and would be loved fain,*
> *But am betrothed unto Your enemy;*
> *Divorce me, untie, or break that knot again;*
> *Take me to You, imprison me, for I*
> *Except You enthrall me, never shall be free*
> *Nor ever chaste, except you ravish me.*[41]

Part of celibate living is allowing God to love you in darkness, loneliness and confusion, as well as feeling the embrace of God in times of joy.

Preparing for a Lifetime of Celibacy

Celibacy is both a gift and a skill or discipline. A skill needs to be practiced over and over again. If you join a volleyball team, a debate team, or take piano lessons, you know you have to practice. There are a set of skills to develop with each sport, art or discipline. Along the way we learn by trial and error. We will make mistakes. It takes time to become a healthy, authentic celibate. Just as the athlete practices with intention, so celibacy needs to be practiced intentionally. Just as we would accept criticism and advice in training in sports or music, we need to accept the same from the wisdom figures in our spiritual lives.

---

[41] Donne, John. *Holy Sonnets V.*

I can't imagine anyone successfully living a celibate life without a life of prayer. "To be empty for God" is St. Thomas Aquinas' definition for celibacy. Henry Nouwen points out: "Both [celibacy and prayer] are expressions for being vacant for God…Contemplative prayer is standing naked, powerless and vulnerable before God. God can show us love. We can become free with a real sense of being accepted, not totally alone."[42] There is an undifferentiated bond between our prayer, celibacy, and poverty. Religious celibacy cannot be lived honestly without contemplative prayer and poverty of spirit. As Nouwen said, "Celibate lifestyle asks for voluntary poverty. A wealthy celibate is like a fat sprinter. Anyone serious about celibacy will not live, eat, drink better than those to whom they are sent."[43] Being sexually alive and celibate confronts us with our weakness, poverty and dependence on God. We desire to be empty for God, to experience God in prayer, and yet the emptiness frightens us. A verse from Psalm 16 has helped me deal with the reality: "You, God, are all I have and you give me all I need. My life is in your hands. How wonderful are your gifts!"

It is important to cultivate discipline in your life. Create at least one discipline that you do every day. This could be 15 minutes of centering prayer or a walk. Commit yourself to a daily discipline. It will bear fruit later in unexpected skills. In a reference to wisdom, we read in the Old Testament, "From your youth embrace discipline; thus will you find wisdom with graying hair. As though plowing and sowing, draw close to her; then await her bountiful crops. For in cultivating her you will labor but little, and soon you will eat of her fruits…Put your feet into her fetters, and your neck under her yoke. Stoop your shoulders and carry her…

---

[42] "Celibates Need Prayer and Poverty," *Vision '96.* Bery Publishing Services, Evanston, IL.

[43] *Ibid.*

with all your soul draw close to her; with all your strength keep her ways. Search her out, discover her; seek her and you will find her. Search her out, discover her; seek her and you will find her. Then when you have her do not let her go; thus will you afterward find rest in her, and she will become your joy" (Sirach 6: 18 – 29).

Honoring and cultivating beauty through music, art, poverty, drama or one of the arts will lift your celibate lifestyle out of self and insert you more into a reality than can be transforming. In *Care of the Soul*, Thomas More writes about the soul's need to be nurtured by the beautiful. If you have a struggle with a particular problem, you might want to engage in an activity that lifts you up and out of yourself. Try listening to music, hiking in the mountains, walking the beach or gazing at an icon. Focus on beauty.

Where does beauty or the arts have a place in your life? If you can draw, paint, play an instrument, compose, or write, you may find a creative outlet for your sexual energy. As some say: "If you don't spend it (sexual energy), it will spend you!" Exercise is another healthy way to deal with sexual energy. It is not that sexual tension will disappear by working out or training for a marathon, but running might make it manageable.

How can you begin to prepare now for a celibate life? First, realize this means much more than abstaining from sexual activity. An active, healthy prayer life is a must. Good peer relationships and support system of friends is also necessary. Do you have people you can have fun with? Is there anyone you can trust with your secrets? Whom do you listen to? Who trusts you? Developing good intimacy skills will prepare you for ministry and community. Learning when and where you can appropriately confide your personal story is a basic intimacy skill. The ability to say,

"I'm uncomfortable with this gesture or expression," or "No" shows signs of mature assertiveness. Expressing anger, sadness, joy and affection keep unhealthy dynamics from building up from within. Developing mutuality in relationships demands give and take, time to listen and time to speak, reaching out and drawing back.

Knowing yourself will enable you to be a more authentic lover. What is your passion? Your dream? How can you be pure of heart and single-hearted in the present day? Ask yourself this question: Do I know *whose* I am, to whom I belong? Honesty with self alerts us to be other centered. When you listen to someone, try to identify with their feelings and situation. Active listening will stretch your ears and heart for pastoral ministry. Focusing outward on people's needs will give your vocation some direction other than self preoccupation. When is the last time you did a favor for someone? Hopefully you are someone that others feel free to ask for help.

Knowing your sexual orientation, your sexual patterns and rhythm of tension is part of responding authentically. When you know where you are most vulnerable, you have a head start on being faithful. What pulls you down? Or in other language, what are your "near occasions of sin?" Is there anything that controls you or leaves you un-free? A healthy balance is one in which you trust your instincts and respect your bodily sexuality as a gift from God. In trusting your instincts, you will be alert to situations in which "something is not freeing here." Reflecting on your sexual history will help you find wisdom by honestly facing your experiences, digesting them, and learning to integrate them into the whole of your life. Sexual identity is a developmental process. We must go through stages of coming to understand ourselves, knowing how we respond, and knowing who we are attracted to.

The ability to set limits grows with this self knowledge. When you know where you are most likely to go overboard in life, you will more easily recognize the pitfalls. Can you say "No" to people when it is appropriate to do so? If someone bothers you, can you say, "When you do such and such...I feel...?" Can you set limits in your spending, service to others, expression of affection and self-gratifying activities? Impulse control is essential for healthy celibacy. It is the ability not to react to stimuli and instead to reflect responsibly aware of the consequences. The mere click of a computer can lead some people into a world of pornography which is too easily accessible.

The two most crucial abilities for celibate living seem to be on opposite ends of a continuum: the ability to enjoy solitude and the support of good friendships. Can you creatively use time alone, or are you in need of constant companionship? Do you enjoy your own company? A little at a time, learn what your inner resources are. Do you have a few good friends who you can trust, have fun with and celebrate with? What is your capacity for solitude and for relationship? The answer to this last question will give you the indication of the quality of your celibate life.

Religious have the support of community in living the vowed life. Diocesan priests often belong to support groups in which they receive affirmation, challenge, support and friendship. We cannot do it alone!

Work at a holistic health plan which includes setting clear physical, intellectual, emotional, social and spiritual goals. Pay attention to your body. Giving your body legitimate comfort can safeguard you from guilt-free binges (because you "deserve" them). Do you overwork, overeat, or over drink when you are lonely? Can you delay gratification? Celibacy calls for Olympian delayed gratification skills. On the other hand, in *Christotherapy*, the Jesuit Bernard Tyrell recommends habits of mind-fasting and spirit feasting.[44] As celibates, we can still enhance our lives by reverence for the sensual and aesthetic. The arts, music, and beauty are ways of spirit feasting and feeding the soul. Mind-fasting involves the discipline of monitoring which fantasies I feed and those I fast from. Mind-fasting calls me to watch where my mind wanders when it's free. Fantasy can be healthy as well as harmful. You will know your fantasies by the fruit they bear!

Another area for reflection is that of your attitude towards heterosexuality and homosexuality. Science, medicine and psychology are presenting us with new information everyday about the reality of sexual orientation. One theory suspects that sexual orientation might be identifiable from the womb. Autopsies performed at UCLA on the brains of gay males gave evidence of a possible genetic predisposition to homosexuality. Know your own sexual journey and prejudices *before* you apply to a seminary or religious community.

For most religious communities and dioceses, it does not matter what your sexual orientation is, as long as you are able and plan to commit to a celibate lifestyle. Vocation directors will want to see skills for celibacy already in place when you apply. Usually there is a requirement of lived celibacy for two years or so before application. The skills mentioned above will all be considered. If you are homosexual, and live an exclusively gay lifestyle, even though celibate, you will want to work on developing an inclusive social circle. If you are heterosexual, you will want to monitor any condescending or derogatory attitudes towards your opposite sex and any homophobic tendencies. No matter what

---

[44] NY: Seabury Press. 1975. Chapter IV: "Mind-fasting and Spirit Feasting," pp. 73 – 105.

VOCATIONS ANONYMOUS

your sexual orientation, it is important that you are at peace with who you are so that it is not the first thing on your mind whenever you introduce yourself. Sexual orientation, when well integrated, does not define who you are. You are much more than your sexual orientation! To repeat: we go through developmental stages. If you are homosexual it will help to have gone through stages of anger and the need to politicize this issue before entering a formation program.

Particular Issues for Heterosexual persons:	Particular Issues for Homosexual Persons:
Sexist or macho attitudes	Acceptance and peace with one's sexual orientation
Healthy boundaries with the opposite sex	Inclusive lifestyle
Leisure habits that are reflective of intentional celibacy; chaste living	Boundary setting; chaste living
Appropriate expressions of affection	Appropriate expressions of affection
Homophobia	Respect for the opposite sex

Dangers of Celibacy

One of the dangers of celibacy has been mentioned already – selfishness. Some of the other dangers than can slowly creep into celibate living are:

• Avoidance of intimacy

• Living outside of and unaware of one's body

108

SEXUALLY ALIVE AND CELIBATE

- Finding security in "knowing the right answer"

- Over extension

Over extension is the tendency to lose oneself in work or activity. This can be an escape from dealing with feelings and sexual tension. Anything left undigested or un-integrated will come back to haunt you. Shoving feelings and energy aside and not paying attention will complicate life. Failure to develop supportive and healthy friendships will also prevent growth into authentic celibacy. Celibacy is in danger when there is a failure to prayerfully reflect and process what is going on in life.

A safeguard for celibacy is having a "truthsayer" in your life.[45] A danger to celibacy is keeping secrets and living a double life. Having someone who knows all of the chapters of your life can help you to be honest with yourself in the living out of celibacy. Honesty with a spiritual director and/or confessor is also an asset.

Video Rental Ideas[46]

Therese, Diary of a Country Priest, The Mission, Romero, Babette's Feast (Orion, 1987); *City of Joy* (Tri Star, Columbia, 1992); *Brother Sun, Sister Moon* (Paramount Communication Co., 1973); *Ghandi* (Columbia Pictures, 1983); *Thornbirds* (Warner Home Video, 1983); *At Play in the Fields of the Lord* (MCA Universal, 1991); *The Mission* (Warner Brothers, 1986); *Black Robe* (Vidmark, Samuel Goldwyn Home Entertainment, 1991).

---

[45] Fr. Michael Jamail, Unpublished remark.

[46] List compiled with suggestions from Roland Claver, OSFS; Judy Zielinski, OSF; Greg Friedman, OFM; John Malich, FMS; and Henry Herx.

Books to Read

Clarke, OFM Cap., Keith. Being Sexual and Being Celibate: An Experience of Celibacy. Notre Dame, IN: Ave Marie Press. 1982.

Crosby, Michael. Celibacy

Huddleston, Mary Anne. Celibacy Loving: Encounter in Three Dimensions. NY: Paulist Press. 1984.

Nouwen, Henri. Lifesigns: Intimacy, Fecundity, and Ecstasy in Christian Perspective. NY: Doubleday. 1989.

Tyrell, Thomas. Urgent Longings: Reflections on Infatuation, Intimacy, and Sublime Love. Mystic, Conn.: Twenty-Third Publications. 1994.

Whitehead, James and Evelyn. A Sense of Sexuality. NY: Image Publications. 1994.

For Healing of Sexual Abuse

Bass, Ellen and David, Laura. The Courage to Heal. 3rd. edition, NY: Harper Perennial. 1994.

Engel, Beverly. The Right to Innocence: Healing the Trauma of Childhood Sexual Abuse. Los Angeles: J.P. Tarcher. 1989.

Grubman – Black, Stephen. Broken Boys, Mending Men: Recovering from Childhood Sexual Abuse. NY: Ivy Books. 1992.

Lew, Mike. Victims No Longer: Men Recovering from Incest and other Sexual Child Abuse. NY: Perennial Library. 1990.

PART III
SEARCHING

This section of the handbook deals with some practical aspects of visiting religious communities or diocesan offices, as well as the specifics of applying to religious communities or seminaries.

VOCATIONS ANONYMOUS

Chapter seven

FEAR OF FAILURE

One obstacle to entering the novitiate or the seminary might be the fear of failure. Taking the steps to apply to a diocese or religious order and going through the process is time and energy consuming. Moving into a formation program is leaving the "world" you know and calls for courage. You invest a considerable amount of time, courage and energy to enter!

What if you discover after a few weeks or months that religious life is **not** for you? Or after a few years? Perhaps you fear facing your family and friends who may view leaving as failure. These are real concerns for adults who leave one familiar world behind in order to enter an unknown one. In some cultures, shame and embarrassment may accompany a sense of failure.

Is it failure? According to the Church, a person who leaves has **not** failed. The purpose of a novitiate or seminary is to enable a person to further discern God's will and to test the "fit." If you are not happy or healthy in a formation program, then God is probably calling you elsewhere.

Formation is **not** a test you pass or fail; it is the place you discover if a certain way of life suits you with your particular temperament, background, and gifts. A vocation to priesthood or religious life needs confirmation.

Confirmation comes during the formation process when you sense you could be your best self in a specific religious community or in the diocesan priesthood. It is a mutual discernment. The diocese or religious order also concurs that you *are* suitable, can work well and live in their particular lifestyle and vocation.

In the first chapter, *vocation* was referenced as a "conversation with God."[47] This conversation continues. The direction the conversation takes may surprise you. The challenge is for you to stay in conversation. That means being faithful to prayer, being honest with a spiritual director and being open to any shifts in the dialogue. By entering into the conversation you manifest openness to God's will. Even if at times you experience silence, tension, or confusion, the call to fidelity challenges you to "hang in there."

Taking time out in your life for discernment will benefit you for the rest of your life. Whether you give a year to discerning God's will, or actually enter a formation program, you gain. Discernment is a win/win situation. A period of serious discernment and/or formation will enable you to:

- Learn more about your Catholic faith and spirituality

- Deepen your relationship with God

- Learn more about yourself

- Make new friends with others also discerning (a group of people who may share your faith, values and confusion!)

What a wonderful opportunity it is to have "time off" in our life to learn more about yourself, God, Church, and ministry in a formation program.

---

[47] *Ibid.* Whitehead, p. 6.

In my twenty-one years of ministry as a vocation director, I never met a man or a woman who entered and left the community/seminary who said they were sorry they spent time in formation. No one has ever said to me, "I wasted a year of my life," or, "It was a terrible mistake." Instead, I hear from ex-seminarians and ex-postulants and novices stories of friendships formed for life, of new understandings of their Catholic faith, of a more intimate relationship with God, and of personal growth.

Looking at this from another perspective, time in a formation program is comparable to the time some young adults in other churches give to a type of novitiate. Mormons spend two years in mission where they pray, minister and live celibately. Every Buddhist spends time living as a monk before entering into marriage. Instead of fearing failure, readjust your perspective to envision the rich possibilities that await you in a formation program, whether or not you stay.

Failure is not always bad in itself. Jesus experienced failure in his life when not all who heard him believed what he proclaimed. To some, Jesus seemed a failure because of his suffering and death on the cross. His 33 years of life and work may not have appeared "successful," but they were meaningful. In one of the exercises presented on the 30 Day Ignatian Exercises, St. Ignatius encourages the retreatant to pray for insults, poverty, and failure in the context of Jesus' experience. It is a difficult prayer. So if you fear failure, remember who has gone before you and the life that sprang up out of the seeming failures!

If fear of failure is keeping you from entering, then you might want to look at two aspects of yourself, your imagination, and your trust barometer.

VOCATIONS ANONYMOUS

Kierkegaard wrote, "Fear is the daughter of the imagination." I often find that most of my fears are never realized. I waste energy worrying about things that never happen. My imagination is very active and creative. What if this happens? What if I don't have what I need? Some common fears about priesthood / religious life are:

- I'm afraid that they'll try to fit me into a mold, or change my personality.

- I'm afraid that I'll lose my independence and not be treated as an adult or be free to make my own decisions.

- I'm afraid I'll be so busy that I'll give and give and then burnout.

- I'm afraid that I'll fall in love with somebody.

- I'm afraid that I'm not good enough, holy enough, worthy enough.

- I'm afraid that there may be nobody left in the order when I grow old.

An example from my own life may illustrate this dynamic of fear. I used to give piano recitals. Part of performing is memorizing hundreds of pages of musical scores. Just before I sat down to begin a recital, I imagined forgetting where I was going in the middle of a three-part Bach fugue! The more I gave into my imagination, the more likely I was to forget. My imagination fed my fear. The only antidote was to gently dismiss the thought and put my trust in the people praying for me and in the endless hours of practicing and preparing.

One of St. Ignatius' Rules for Discernment of Spirits is to go against the inclination that leads to desolation. In Latin, this is called "agere contra." I suggest that you go against the fear of failure and focus on trusting God, your goodness, your instinct, and the time you've invested in discernment. Instead of feeding your fear with imaginative thoughts, focus on God who is working in you and through you. Make an act of trust!

Many of the saints experimented with new lifestyles, ministry and vision. Most of them were never seen as a success in their lifetime. They may have thought they failed miserably. Only later did the Church acknowledge their unique contribution, their insights and vision. During Joan of Arc's life, the spectators may have viewed her life as a failure. Similarly, Blessed Mother Teresa was asked once if she felt her ministry was successful in light of the world's many poor, hungry, and abandoned people. She replied that God does not call us to be successful, but to be faithful.

Being faithful means that we stay in the conversation with God. If in our praying and discerning we hear a call to leave the seminary or convent, then surely it is not a failure, but a matter of being faithful. We take one step at a time. All God asks of us is to say "yes" today, and again each new day. It is not a matter of "staying"; it is a matter of daily living faithfully by responding to **God's** call.

Some Scriptures to Ponder

"For I know well the plans I have in mind for you, says the Lord, plans for your welfare, not for woe! Plans to give you a future full of hope. When you call me, when you go to pray to me, I will listen to you. When you look for me, you will find me. Yes, when you seek me with all your heart, you will find me with you, says the Lord, and I will change your lot."[48]

[48] Jeremiah 29: 11 – 14 New American Bible.

VOCATIONS ANONYMOUS

Deuteronomy 1: 30 – 31; 2: 7

Psalms 23, 62, 139

John 14: 16 – 28

Ephesians 3: 14 – 21

Philippians 3: 7 – 21 and 4: 4 – 13

Some of Carlo Carretto's books have helped me with the fear of failure. Perhaps some excerpts from his writings may help you in your meditation. Due to the time these words were written, the language is not inclusive. These are quoted as is.

"God goes before me. He went before Abraham, Moses, David…and in order to make them understand that it was He Himself who was acting, calling, bringing to life, he led them to the limit of their poverty…for Abraham by Sarah's barrenness, for David by the humiliation he endured in his horrible sin…God always leads man to his limit so that he may understand and enjoy the Good News…that God is God, God of the Impossible…God is greater than his call. What matters is to walk towards his presence and be certain in faith that it is he who is leading us."

"Our weakness is that we look at ourselves, always at ourselves, only at ourselves. We do not realize that our mother is at hand and that God is the mother in whom we live and have our being. And that he will bring us out into the light. I am the poor God's child in the womb of the dark generating process, who cries out his limitations and incapacity."

"Have you understood, brother, what I've been trying to say this evening? Do not be afraid when God calls you, but do not be afraid when he is silent. Do not be afraid

118

when he asks you to perform some task, but do not be afraid when He asks for it back. Do not be afraid if He gives you a husband or a wife, but do not be afraid if He doesn't. God is greater than His call. God is greater than your works. God is greater than the good we do. What matters is to walk towards His presence and to be certain in faith that it is He who is leading us."[49]

---

[49] Carretto, Carlo. *Desert in the City.* NY: Crossroad, 1982.

VOCATIONS ANONYMOUS

Chapter eight

HOW TO EXPLORE RELIGIOUS ORDERS AND THE DIOCESAN PRIESTHOOD

Huge telephone book sized catalogues and endless websites sometimes intimidate people who are discerning a vocation to priesthood or religious life. If you have ever browsed through the internet, directories, guides to religious orders, or catalogues of vocation advertisements, then the exposure to so many different options and possibilities has probably made you feel a bit overwhelmed.

It is difficult enough to discern a call to be priest, sister or brother. So perhaps you have prayed and discerned that God is calling you to priesthood or religious life; but where? Could these be some of your questions?

- Am I called to be a sister or brother in a contemplative or an active order?

- Which order?

- How will I know?

- Am I called to be a diocesan priest, or a priest that belongs to a religious community?

- Where do I start?

Let me offer some suggestions for dealing with this quandary.

121

First of all, some definitions are in order. There are different types of communities in which people live out their baptismal call.

The person in a *religious community* takes vows, serves, lives and prays in community and follows the constitutions and rule of the order. Each religious order is a gift to the Church. Each was founded for a specific purpose. This distinctive purpose and gift is called the *charism* of the order. It is the key to understanding the order's particular lifestyle and mission. After Vatican II, most communities struggled to put their charism into a single phrase or sentence so that their particular mission could be clarified and better understood. Decisions and choices are made within the context of the religious order's spirit, charism, customs and constitutions.

A *diocesan priest* is called to serve the local church through parish ministry, although some priests may for a time teach, do retreat work, counseling, or other forms of diocesan service. The diocesan priest makes promises of obedience and celibacy to his bishop. He does not take vows. The diocesan priest does not take the vow of poverty or live in community life with rules and a constitution describing his lifestyle. His life's ministry is within the boundaries of a particular diocese. Through parish leadership, preaching, and sacramental ministry, the diocesan priest journeys through life from the "womb to the tomb" with parishioners. Often small groups of diocesan priests will meet regularly to pray and lend support in living out their priesthood.

A *religious priest* belongs to an order in which he takes vows. He usually lives in community and his lifestyle and mission are shaped by the particular charism of the community in ways similar to sisters and brothers.

HOW TO EXPLORE

A *brother* is a vowed man who lives religious life in community. Brothers serve in a variety of ministries, as was noticed in the previous chapter. He is not ordained. It is *not* because he chooses what some perceive as a secondary choice to priesthood but because he feels *called to be a brother*. Since he is called to community, it is an insult to ask him, "Why didn't you go all the way and get ordained?" Brothers are too often left out of the church vocation conversations, and not recognized for the amazing contributions that they make to the church and to society.

Monastic life centers around periods of liturgical prayer. The *active religious* organize their day around the demands of ministry.

A *secular institution* is a form of consecrated life in which lay people take vows. They do not live together or wear habits. They manage their own finances and have no single apostolate. They take part in a formation program to prepare for vows and develop a regular prayer life.

There are *ecclesial movements* in the Church emerging all the time that gather vowed and mostly non vowed members for the sake of the mission, to form them in the spirituality of the movement and support them in their lives. Focolare, the St. Egidio, the Christian Life movement, the Catholic Worker Movement begun by Venerable Dorothy Day (hopefully to be a canonically recognized Saint soon!). Some members take private vows. Pope Benedict XVI invited members of lay ecclesial movements to "Be builders of a better world, according to the 'ordo amoris' (order of love) in which the beauty of human life is expressed."[50]

A *third order* is an organization of men and women who gather regularly to learn about the spirituality of the partic-

---

[50] Letter to Participants of the 2nd World Meeting of Ecclesial Movements and New Communities, Benedict XVI.

123

ular order to which they are associated. They also participate in a formation program before making a commitment. The members live in their own homes and maintain their own jobs. Prayer and service usually characterize members of third orders.

Doing Your Homework First

Before you begin exploring religious communities it is important that you do some of your own homework first. The first part of this section will offer some suggestions for doing that inner homework. The second part will give you some suggestions for ways of exploring your options.

Knowing yourself and your values is important before you look for a home in a religious community or diocese. Take a personal inventory. Examine the call you are experiencing, preferably with the help of a spiritual director. It will help to have someone with whom you can articulate the call. At first, that call may seem as a vague, indescribable yearning for something more, a heartfelt sense that God is asking something of you. An authentic call comes from God through your baptism and through your parish community. It is confirmed through people who affirm, encourage, and invite you to think about a vocation. The call to priesthood and religious life does not happen outside the context of the faith community. A call to priesthood is not a private deal between God and yourself.

What do people say to you about your vocation? The person you are now, with your particular gifts, qualities, talents, and spirituality, is a clue that can lead you to the diocese or community that will eventually be your home.

Write down in your journal what would be most important to you in living out your baptismal call as a sister, priest

HOW TO EXPLORE

or brother. Prioritize those values, practices and vision. One way to approach this task is to imagine if you were founding a religious order, or living as a diocesan priest, how you would design the lifestyle, prayer, and focus of this particular vocation.

Fr. Anthony de Mello, SJ, has a prayer exercise in *Sadhana* called "Holy Desires." One prayerful approach is to spend time getting in touch with your dreams, your holy desires. When Jesus looks you in the eye and asks, "What is it that you really desire?" as he asked in the first chapter of John, what do you say?

You might also take an inventory of your strengths, your spirituality, gifts, and talents. Spirituality is the personal style in which you relate to God and live out your faith. Here are some examples:

1. My Spirituality is based on a reverence for creation as God's gift to us. In the spirit of Francis of Assisi, I feel called to promote a sacred ecology. I often experience God's presence through nature.

2. The heart of my spirituality is the Eucharist. I feel called to spend quality time before the Blessed Sacrament. Scripture also is important in my life. I spend time each day quietly reading my bible and meditating.

3. I am excited about God's love. I want to share that love with other people who have not yet discovered how good God is. I experience God's presence in our prayer group, young adult group, and in the retreats we give.

4. I am disturbed by the injustices in the world and feel a passion to do something about it, to work for systemic change for those who are oppressed, to be a voice for the voiceless, to preach the Gospel by fighting to change the

125

VOCATIONS ANONYMOUS

structures in government and society that keep people in poverty and slavery.

Here are some examples of what might be listed in the inventory of your strengths, gifts and qualities:

- *Compassion and prudence* (People feel free to open up to me without fear of being judged).

- *Prayerfulness* (I recognize God in daily life).

- *Talent for organization* (I can put on programs, organize and serve with humility and joy).

- *Strength of my convictions and passion to make changes in our world* (I can articulate well what I believe and I am an active Christian).

- *Adaptability, flexibility* (I can be at home with people of various cultural backgrounds).

As you reflect and pray about this inner call, spend time listening to what God has to say. God communicates through quiet prayer time, through scripture, the Eucharist, nature, other people, and the events of our lives. Keep track of what has the most impact on you. Which events, phrases from scripture, or comments from friends pierce through you? God speaks to us in our daily lives in a myriad of ways. Jot down these experiences. They may provide a clearer direction in your search for a community or diocese that resonates with who you are.

Some good questions for you to answer for yourself might be:

- Where do you find life? What is most life-giving for you now?

HOW TO EXPLORE

- What is there about you that an order or diocese would welcome? Which gifts do you bring?

- What about you might be troublesome for an order or diocese?

- Do you now live simply? How do you live celibately now?

- How would you adapt to living in community?

Which Way?

Depending on your experience, you may or may not have a sense about the type of religious life or priesthood God is calling you to. Here's a quick way to get in touch with your leanings toward a specific vocation. List these words on a sheet of paper, leaving spaces between each one:

For Men: hermit – monk – parish priest – active apostolic brother – religious order priest – missionary priest – missionary brother

For Women: cloistered contemplative – monastic religious – missionary sister – active religious – traditional form of religious life – evolving form of religious life

Now spontaneously write one word associations for each category. Without censoring, jot down any images, feelings, or descriptive phrases about that particular vocation. For example, under "missionary," you might respond: adventurous, challenging, difficult, poor, dangerous. Under "hermit" you might write: lonely, too quiet, far removed, prayerful, penitential. Again, these are only personal reactions and not necessarily the reality for all people.

Look over the list. Can you identify yourself with any of

127

those associations? Which one of these would be closest to who you are, to who you feel called to become?

Some Prerequisites for Entering

Every diocese or religious community has its own requirements for acceptance of candidates. You will want to ask about them as you explore. Here are some of the basic expectations that most seminaries and formation programs require.

Most orders and seminaries require that you enter free of all debt, including student loans. However, since more and more applicants have student loans, NRVC (National Religious Vocation Conference) has done a study and offered suggestions and ways to alleviate those debts incurred from study. Family obligations, such as the care of a parent, need to be taken care of ahead of time.

Most communities and dioceses require two years of *intentional* celibacy before entrance. It is expected that a candidate receive the sacraments regularly, pray, and have an ability to talk about faith. Good physical, emotional, and spiritual health is also often a requirement, as well as a demonstration of the openness to learn. You must also have received all the sacraments of Initiation – Baptism, Eucharist and Confirmation.

If you haven't thought about any of these before, you might begin working on them now. Sometimes the vocation director may ask you to get counseling, or to work on personal issues before entering. This would be to your advantage, not a reason to dismiss one group and run to another that will take you right away. The personal issues will only be there to "haunt" you later on. Try to see the invitation to growth as one coming from God.

Preparing to Visit Communities or Dioceses

Once you have done the homework of personal reflection, you will be better prepared to visit communities. Compare your search to the real estate business. If you want to rent an apartment or buy a house, you go looking with some of your own needs in mind. Before you start exploring religious orders or diocese, you want to have a sense of self, and of your own values and call.

One of the first choices you will encounter is that between contemplative and active vocations. The focus of the contemplative is prayer. That is not to say that active religious and diocesan priests are not contemplatives. Neither is it true to say that contemplatives are not in ministry of service to the Church. I know many busy priests and religious who are genuinely contemplative people. I also know cloistered contemplatives who carry the needs and reality of the world with them prayerfully each day.

Some common myths about the cloistered contemplative life are:

- You have to be an introvert to be a contemplative. NOT!

- Anyone in a cloister is out of touch with the world! NOT!

- The more loud, vivacious and funny the person is, the less s/he is called to the cloistered! NOT!

If any of the above is your reason for dismissing the idea of a cloistered, contemplative life, you better look again! Another mistaken notion is that if one lacks social skills, or exhibits uneasiness with people, the contemplative vocation is the choice for him or her. NOT! Contemplatives are free women and men, and don't identify their lives as "confined." Contemplatives also enjoy life, affection, nature, and are some of the most down to earth, practical, common sense people I know. They are not usually people who have had remarkable visions; rather they are faithful community members, thinking of others and praying for the needs of the world. You'll hear laughter when you visit! Most bishops, when founding new dioceses, ask for a contemplative community to come to the diocese because they know that the contemplative communities are powerhouses of prayer.

As you discern, ask yourself where the desire and the energy is when you think about your future as a priest or religious.

If you are drawn to the active life, you may find energy in imagining yourself going out to people, to the "marketplace" with the good news. Propelled by a prayer life, a person moves out into ministry – teaching, preaching, pastoring, celebrating the sacraments, nursing, etc.

Energy for the contemplative cloistered vocation is often found in the desire to live a life of prayer and penance as a service to the Church and the entire world – to live a life hidden with Christ in God.

Given your background and particular personality, do you feel called to the cloister, or to an active ministerial life? Over time, use your imagination to fantasize about following a contemplative vocation, then switch, and dream about what your life would look like in an active community. Where is the most enthusiasm? That enthusiasm is a good indicator of where you may belong.

At some stage in your discernment, whether you feel called to the cloistered contemplative life or not, I suggest that you visit one of these communities. Go to the Carmelites, Poor Clares, Dominicans, Benedictines, Trappistines,

HOW TO EXPLORE

Trappists or Camaldolese, and ask them to pray for you in your discernment. It's a good investment!

Reading about religious orders and the lives of the saints, or perusing contemporary periodicals on Catholic spirituality and life, can help you learn about church vocations. Don't move forward with misinformation you might have accrued over the years from myths, stereotypes, or Hollywood images of priests or religious. Part of the discernment process is gathering data and getting accurate information.

The People You Know

Begin with the priests and religious you know and feel comfortable talking to (an email contact for a sister, brother or priest, your parish priest, a religious you knew growing up or at school). Ask if you could talk to them seriously about a church vocation.

The Vocation Office

Call the vocation office and ask for an appointment to see the vocation director. Some vocation directors are full time; others may have limited time because of other responsibilities. Expect to be asked some questions over the phone before the appointment is set. Some offices have directories and information on the religious communities working the diocese. You will be able to get feedback, information and direction regarding church vocations. You may also plug into the vocation discernment programs offered. The NCD-VD, National Conference of Diocesan Vocation Directors, can let you know how to contact your local vocation director at *www.ncdvd.org* or (631) 645-8210 If you are looking at religious life, contact NRVC, National Religious Vocation

131

Conference at (773) 363 5454 or *www.nrvc.net*. You can find both conferences on Facebook!

Directories of Religious Communities

Browse through a directory with a highlighter (if the book is your personal copy). If a particular word, phrase, value or charism leaps out at you while reading the description of a religious order or diocesan lifestyle, then highlight it. It is not wise to try to read through a directory all at once. Periodically, continue browsing and highlighting. Later on, when you flip through the pages, you may notice an emerging pattern of values, charisms, or spirits that resonate with you. This will also help you learn about different vocations.

Some magazines, like *Vocations and Prayer*, *Guide to Religious Ministries*, and *Vision Magazine*, and *Oye* carry advertisements for communities. Many religious communities and dioceses have websites that provide a rich source of information. Explore *www.vocation-network.org* which offers a Vocation Match, Q and A and a quiz. Use a web browser, search key words like "Catholic vocations," or "Catholic priest, sister or brother." If you are interested in a particular order, search under the name of that order. YouTube offers great resources for exploring religious life and priesthood. You have to use your intelligent filters as I suspect some are "actors" and there could be an agenda attached to the video.

Contact the communities or diocesan seminaries that appeal to you. If you write or email, keep it brief, ask for more information, and inquire about the possibility of visiting a nearby convent, residence or seminary. If you phone, ask for an appointment to see the vocation contact person in a community near you.

Visit the Community or Diocesan Seminary

Personal contact, face to face with those who belong to the diocese or community you are exploring is the best way to begin. When you meet the vocation director, ask if it is possible to pray, eat or socialize with the members of the community. As you visit, you may want to be aware of whether or not you feel at home with the group. Apart from the inevitable initial shyness and anxiety, you may notice that you feel more at home in some places than in others.

Questions to Ask

When visiting, you may wonder what to talk about. You will also be asked questions about yourself. Discernment is a mutual process. A vocation director will be interested in the whole of your life – not only the part that you will label "spiritual." You will be asked about your age, educational background, job, relationships, family, service and involvement with community or parish.

You are free to ask questions too.

What is the charism of the community? A charism is that particular gift that a religious community or diocesan priest lives. The charism will give you a sense of this particular community's purpose and meaning. You might want to ask how the community lives out the charism in its current ministries. Other questions you might ask include:

- How do you live community life together?

- What ministries are you involved in?

- How do you pray together? What's the emphasis in your prayer life?

- What do you look for in an applicant to their community or diocese?

If you have done the inner work suggested in Part I, your questions will flow from what is most important to you. For example, if being with the poor and working with the poor is one of your values, then ask how the community lives an option for the poor. The same follows for the spirituality, sense of Church and desire for community life.

Some general questions about how the vows are lived will be determined by your values. For example, if you have developed some strong friendships that you hope to maintain in your new lifestyle, you will want to ask if friendships outside the community are encouraged. Some orders may ask you to make a break from those relationships.

Poverty

How are personal needs met? How is budgeting handled? Are members required to ask permission for basic needs? How are members accountable to one another?

How does the group communally express their vow of poverty?

Are the members expected to engage only in ministries that pay a stipend or salary?

Celibacy

What kind of preparation and education is there for chaste celibate living? Are friendships outside the community allowed or encouraged? Is the body viewed as a gift or as a hindrance to holiness? What is the policy of the community or diocese with regards to homosexuality? How does bonding take place in the community? What mechanisms are in place to promote community?

Obedience

How are decisions made about ministry and work assignments?

Is there a process for choosing leadership? Is dialogue and consultation part of decision making?

Ministry

How are members prepared for ministry?

You would *not* want to ask all of these questions on your first visit or communication. They would feel on trial! The more sensitive questions could be brought up later on if you pursue a discernment process with them.

How a community does ministry varies depends on the charism. Mother Teresa's sisters, the Missionaries of Charity, give direct service to the poor by attending the dying on the streets, feeding the hungry, and providing shelter for the homeless. The Sisters of Social Service are engaged in legislative efforts to fight for more just benefits and conditions for the poor in our society. Their founder, Margaret Slachta, said that some may dry the tears of the poor, but "my sisters will work to prevent injury being inflicted in the first place." "We are to be pioneers of a better world, working for social reform." Sr. Simone Campbell was being faithful to this charism as she hit the road with *Nuns on the Bus.* Both Mother Teresa and Margaret Slachta's communities serve the poor, but in different ways.

Each community incarnates the gospel with a focus on

VOCATIONS ANONYMOUS

a specific aspect of Jesus' message. This may not necessarily happen just through ministry, but also through the community's mission, or way of being present to the world. For example, Jesuit spirituality aims at finding God in all things. Benedictines treasure the liturgy in Eucharist and Divine Office as well as the rhythm of work and prayer in daily life. Dominicans strive to reflect truth in their preaching, and value lifelong education and study. As you explore spiritualities, which resonate with your own?

Sometimes the community logo, symbol, or emblem will reveal a lot about the order's focus. Notice the language used as the religious describe themselves.

You may also want to find out some basic statistics regarding the community. How many are in the formation program? What is the median age? Which countries are they located in? How many belong to this particular community or diocese?

Diocesan Priesthood

There are some special considerations for those looking at diocesan priesthood. The call to diocesan priesthood comes from God, often through the local parish community. It is confirmed in the local church, and after ordination it is in the local church in which the priest serves.

- What support systems are available for the diocesan clergy?

- What are the educational requirements for the seminary?

- Does the diocese have its own seminary? Where do the seminarians study?

HOW TO EXPLORE

- What types of ministries are the priests involved in?

- What are the urgent needs of the diocese? What kind of person would make a good priest and be able to help meet some of these needs?

- What kind of living arrangements do the priests have? Are they required to live in the parish rectory, or are other arrangements possible?

- What is the cultural makeup of the Catholic population of the diocese?

After the Visit

After you visit the convent, house of formation, rectory or seminary, it is important that you give yourself some time to reflect on what happened. Spend time mentally going over the visit. In a notebook, write down:

1. What were you attracted to or felt comfortable with when you observed the community or seminary during your visit. (Perhaps you could relate to the way the seminarians joked around together, the camaraderie the brothers had with each other, the way the sisters spoke about the people they worked with.)

2. What you were *not* attracted to or not comfortable with during the visit. (Perhaps you couldn't relate to their focus, the way they prayed together, what the community was interested in, how they interacted.)

Keeping track of visits to communities or seminaries in this reflective process will clarify for you where you are not called as well as where you may be called. Get to know the members of the community. Observe them interacting with each other. Get to know their spirituality and ministry and plot this against your own personal history, personality, and background.

As you reflect, keep in mind that the perfect community or diocese does not exist! Try to distinguish between the very real human imperfections you may see, and even with those imperfections, whether you may be called to join in the community's or the diocesan mission.

Two people visiting the same place could have opposite reactions. Each community is a gift to the Church. There is a colorful diversity in the way religious life is lived in the United States. Communities and dioceses cross the spectrum, from traditional style to those living on the frontiers of an evolving form of religious life for the future. You need to find where you can best be called to be your most authentic self and where you would be most at home. Where would you be truly challenged? All this needs to be done in the context of prayer, reflection and spiritual direction.

Ministry Experience

One of the prerequisites for entering formation for the priesthood or religious life is some experience of serving others. If you are already involved in a parish ministry, such as serving as a teacher, a catechist, a lector, a Eucharistic minister, Catholic worker, on the social justice committee, or a youth leader, this experience will help you discern your call to ministry.

If you feel called to be a parish priest, ask a priest if you could spend a day following him around. Get a first-hand taste of what diocesan priesthood is all about.[51] If there is a

---

[51] National Conference of Diocesan Vocation Directors, 440 W. Neck Road, Huntington, NY 11743. 631-645-8210. *office@ncdvd.org*

seminary near you, arrange to spend a day going to classes with the seminarians, attending liturgy and sharing in meals with them. Ask the seminarians questions about their formation program and lifestyle.

Another fruitful way to explore a community is to spend a day in ministry with a sister, brother or priest. The vocation director can recommend someone who you could "shadow" for a day. This will give you an insight into the vision a community may have for the way it serves others. Observe how the priest or religious interacts and is involved in ministry. Some communities offer a weeklong summer experience of ministering with the community. Others have associate programs that allow you to live in community and minister for about 6 months to a year with the order.[52]

Concluding Thought: God is in Charge

It could be overwhelming to think that you had to go through this process on your own. There are so many religious orders, so much literature, so many choices…but remember that God leads you and guides you. God uses events and other people to help you co-create your future. What may seem like an accidental meeting could well be a providential one. You may have browsed the internet, thumbed through pages of directories and tons of advertisements and brochures and then one day "accidently" meet someone in a grocery store who talks about a particular community or seminary. Keep your exploration in the context of the belief that it is God who providentially leads and guides you. Remember that the process is mutual. The community is also listening to God and will give you honest feedback.

---

[52] Opportunities are listed in *Connections: a Directory of Lay Volunteers Ministry. It gives a description of ministry programs, terms of service, and benefits. Some live in community with religious. For a directory contact the St. Vincent Pallotti Center at 715 Monroe St., N.E., Washington, D.C. 20017-1755 or phone (202) 529-3330.*

Resources

Vision Vocation Guide has a magazine, website and Facebook page. There is also an online Vocation Match that will help you identify the type of community you are looking for. You can order a free hard copy of the magazine as well at:

http://www.vocationnetwork.org/orders

or call Toll-Free: 800-942-2811

Oye, a bilingual vocation magazine, website and Facebook page. Contact them at *www.oyemagazine.org*

Guide to Religious Ministries is available both in book form or online at *http://www.religiousministries.com*. If you prefer a hard copy, copies are available to religious free of charge. Others may purchase a copy directly by sending $10 to:

A Guide to Religious Ministries

210 North Avenue
New Rochelle, NY 10801
For further information, please contact:
914-632-1220 / info@religiousministries.com

Here is the online description:

A Guide to Religious Ministries is the only comprehensive directory of Catholic men's and women's communities in the United States. Search our database to find a men's or women's religious community that could be the right match for you. Whether you wish to become a priest, nun, brother or lay missioner, or just want to find out more about living a religious life, you can discover what these communities offer and the ministries they perform. Additional listings include retreat centers and houses of prayer. You may also search our calendar of events to see if a church, monastery or convent is hosting an event pertaining to vocations. Sending an

HOW TO EXPLORE

inquiry does not obligate you to anything, but it may be the first step toward your life's work.

National Religious Vocation Conference

5420 S. Cornell Avenue, #105
Chicago, Illinois 60615
Phone (773) 363-5454 for a religious vocation director in your area.

Diocesan Vocation Offices often have a listing of communities.

Vocations and Prayer

Subscribe by contacting them at:
info@vocationsandprayer.org / 818-782-1765
http://www.vocationsandprayer.org

VOCATIONS ANONYMOUS

Chapter nine

THE APPLICATION PROCESS (WHAT TO EXPECT)

Applying to a diocesan seminary or religious community requires a lot of time, paperwork and running around to appointments. Each diocese and order has its own required documents and process, but there are some basic requirements. Procuring some documents can take quite a long time. There is no reason you cannot begin rounding them up even before you have made your decision.

The first step will be an interview with the vocation director. If you are ready to apply, you will most likely be given an application packet and an explanation of the process.

Interviews

The vocation director and the team or board will do a lengthy, in depth assessment that may take place over several visits. In religious orders, you will be interviewed by other members of the community, council members, a provincial, or possibly a member of the formation team.

Seminaries have admission teams who interview men who want to study for the priesthood. Usually these interviews are shorter and less comprehensive than the assessment that the vocation director uses. The admission team will probably have seen the assessment and psychological report ahead of time.

You may experience yourself repeating your story and experiences to several people. Expect the process to be thorough and lengthy so that you will hopefully not get too frustrated! There is no *right* answer only the *honest* answer!

Release Forms

You may be asked to sign forms releasing the vocation and formation team, admissions team or provincial council to discuss the information you disclose. Vocation directors will ask for permission to access information from seminaries or religious orders with which you may have had previous association. Sometimes doctors will ask for your signature to release medical findings to the vocation director.

Documents

❐ Baptismal certificate

❐ Certificates for First Communion and Confirmation

❐ Parents' marriage certificate (in some cases, although this is NO LONGER a canonical requirement, thank God!)

❐ Citizenship Information/Immigration Status Verification

❐ Transcripts from high school and colleges

❐ SAT, GRE, and/or MAT scores (in some cases)

❐ Medical, dental and eye examinations

❐ An application form with basic facts, photo, etc.

THE APPLICATION PROCESS

Letters of Recommendation

❒ Pastor of your parish

❒ Former teacher or professor

❒ Past employer(s)

❒ Religious

❒ Former seminary rector

Your spiritual director holds all you say in confidence and therefore cannot be questioned as to your suitability for priesthood or religious life. The Church protects this "internal forum" for the sake of the individual.

Questionnaire and Autobiography

You will be asked to write an autobiography. Depending on your age, the autobiography can range anywhere from three to ten pages.

A questionnaire is sometimes used to ask specific questions about your sense of Church, work history, lifestyle, faith history, financial situation, ministry experience, etc.

Each diocese or order has its own medical forms, application forms, and requirements.

If at any time during the application process you discern an impediment to entering (medical, psychological, financial, etc.) you can stop the process without disclosing information that you prefer to keep private. For example, if your medical exam reveals that you are HIV positive and if there is a policy of not accepting HIV candidates, you could stop the application process without disclosing that information. Inform the doctor, before the lab results are sent back to the

145

vocation director, that you are not continuing the process.

If the psychologist uncovers materials or issues of which you were previously unaware and with which you are uncomfortable, you can withdraw your application.

There are always ways to protect your privacy and dignity.

As a courtesy, if you decide to withdraw your application it is a good idea to inform the vocation director.

The entire process of application can be one of personal growth and awareness, of gratitude in a deeper realization of all that God has done for you and in joyful anticipation of what is to come in your life.

Chapter ten

THE TRIP TO THE PSYCHOLOGIST

All dioceses and almost all religious orders require that you take a psychological test as part of the application process. This can mean anything from taking a No. 2 pencil test of straightforward questions, to a long interview and several pen and paper tests.

Why psychological testing? Just as you will need a recommendation from your pastor or from a religious leader who can attest to your spiritual health, and a report from your doctor regarding your physical condition, you will need a report on your emotional and psychological health as well. The psychological report is used as a screening tool and also as a help in the formation of a person's growth. The psychologist's feedback can enable formation directors to enhance the formation program to include education and experience to help the candidate. In some cases, a diocese or congregation has a legal responsibility to assure the people of God that a person accepted for formation is assessed to be a safe and trustworthy individual from the psychological perspective. Psychological screening is a requirement for the acceptance of a man for priestly studies.

It is natural to fear going to a psychologist for the first time. One's culture may have cultivated certain stereotypes about psychologists or psychological methods. Perhaps you, or people you know, have made judgments about someone

147

who is going to a therapist. Just as no one relishes going to a doctor for a full physical, or to the dentist to get a tooth drilled and filled, so also do people not usually look forward with eagerness to psychological testing!

Information about psychological testing may help to alleviate some of your anxiety.

The Psychologist

The diocese or religious order carefully chooses the psychologists who interview candidates. They ensure that this professional has a respect and reverence for faith and Christian values. You may have heard or read about psychologists who have no regard for one's spiritual experiences, or who may interpret motivations outside of a faith context. This may be true for some, although today there is a growing movement towards the integration of psychology and spirituality. The psychologist chosen by the diocese or community will not discredit your experiences of God, or interpret your call to celibacy as unhealthy or sick!

You may want to ask the vocation director about the particular psychologist who has been recommended to you. You may want to inquire about that person's faith, relative age, marital status, or personality. Feel free to ask the psychologist questions early on in the interview.

The Tests

You will more than likely have a number of tests to take in addition to the interview with the psychologist. Here is a very simple, brief description, from a lay person's view, of some tests you may be asked to take. These are not tests that you can study for, like the GRE or SAT. There are no right answers to these test questions. You answer according to *who you are*. Give the response that spontaneously comes from your gut. Be honest. In order to do so, you must place some confidence in the professional that the vocation director has recommended to you. You will not have to take all of the tests described below. These are samples of what different psychologists use according to their training and preference.

- **MMPI (Minnesota Multiphasic Personality Inventory)**
  This is the most commonly used test. It uses a computer scored answer sheet, like the ones you most likely used in school. You are asked a simple question like: When I was young I used to enjoy playing sports. You answer "true" or "false." The best way to take this test is to trust your first response and not debate in your mind back and forth. This test screens for psychosis. Most vocation directors now ask for the MMPI 2, so your results are measured against other men and women in church ministry.

Personality Tests

- **MBTI (Meyers-Briggs Type Indicator)**
  This is a personality test to see what "type" you are. This test does not screen for mental health. There are 126 questions. You are asked which ways of being, relating and working you most prefer. All 16 personality types it indicates are healthy. It merely indicates preference.

- **WAIS – R (Wechsler Adult Intelligence Scale)**
  An intelligence test using a variety of tasks (blocks, picture completion, sequence of numbers, vocabulary, and comprehension). If you have difficulties with language, or if English is your second language, some of these tests

will more fairly and accurately give a sense of your mental ability.

- **FIRO – B (Fundamental Interpersonal Relations Orientation Behavior)**
  A 54 – item questionnaire intended to measure relational skills.

- **IRAI (Inventory of Religious Activities and Interests – Forms A & B)**
  A paper and pencil test of 240 items. This test measures interests in variety of tasks and occupations.

- **16 PF (Sixteen Personality Factor Questionnaire – Form A)**
  A 180 question test designed to describe 16 dimensions of the personality.

- **Guilford Zimmerman Temperament Survey**
  Answering "yes" or "no" to statements about the style of relating to others, this test examines issues of friendliness, social skills, and intimacy. It contains about 300 items.

- **Personality Research Form E**
  You will rate yourself in this test using either "yes" or "no," or "true" or "false" responses. It covers a wide range of psychological characteristics of achievement, nurturing and impulse. This test is available in Spanish.

Projective Testing

These tests rely on your personal input. You may be given a picture, or series of pictures, and asked to make up a story. You may be shown an inkblot and asked what you see. This type of testing reminds me of the Irish custom of

THE TRIP TO THE PSYCHOLOGIST

reading tea leaves left in the bottom of a cup, or of Charlie Brown looking up at the clouds in the sky to see what they form. When you are presented with images, be as free, imaginative and spontaneous as you can.

- **TAT (Thematic Apperception Test)**
  A series of pictures is presented, and the individual is asked to construct a story or scenario to go along with each series of pictures.

- **Rorschach Inkblots**
  Inkblots on cards are presented so that individual can try to see an image in it and name it. Remember Charlie Brown looking up at the clouds and using his imagination.

- **Rotter Sentence Completion**
  The individual is asked to complete sentences. Answer freely and spontaneously with the first thing that comes to mind. There is no need to impress with eloquent vocabulary. The most ready answer should be given. For example: "When I was a child…"

Other Tests:

- **Personal Problem Checklist for Adults**
  In this test, the individual is asked to simply check-off which are applicable to self.

- **The Interview**
  A long interview with the psychologist will take place after taking the tests. The psychologist will give feedback on the findings and get to know the individual better. Many of the tests can be culturally biased, especially if they are computer scored. They need validation through a person to person interview.

151

**You will NOT have to take all of the above tests
(in case you are feeling overwhelmed at this point)!**

The psychologist will want to know about several different areas of your life. Sometimes the documents you prepare for the vocation director will be a help, i.e., your autobiography, a questionnaire, an assessment by your vocation director.

The areas that you will be asked about in the interview will most likely include:

1. Your faith life, experience of God, Christian service, Christian-based value system

2. Family history, personal background, familiar relationships

3. Personal way of dealing with life, with stress, crisis, leisure preferences, your relationships, emotional life

4. Work history; educational background

5. Your sexual history, preference (orientation), your ability to reach out in love to others; boundary issues

6. Ability to find meaning and value in life

Most likely, you will be asked to tell your story, rather than be asked question after question. In telling your story, many of the questions will be answered.

At any time during the interview you feel uncomfortable about something, tell the psychologist. If you need time to compose yourself, cry, or pause to think, don't hesitate to share that as well.

In order to prepare well for this interview, plan ahead to get a good night's sleep so that you go rested, rather than

THE TRIP TO THE PSYCHOLOGIST

stressed out, so that you present your best self. Plan to give yourself time after the interview to either debrief with a close friend, or to relax and process the experience. Such testing may surface forgotten memories that were joyful or painful. Respect your inner self by saving some time afterwards to rest and reflect on your experience of the interview.

In making an appointment with the psychologist, don't wait until late in the application process. When you first call, you may have to wait a few weeks for an appointment. The first appointment may involve testing. The second appointment will most likely be the interview. It takes the psychologist several weeks to write and send the report to the vocation director. If you have a timeline for your application to a seminary or a religious order, count on at least 4 to 6 weeks between your first appointment and the completed report.

The psychologist should give you feedback about the test and interview findings. Some offer a follow-up appointment so that you will know exactly what the vocation director will hear. You will be affirmed in a summary of your gifts and qualities, as well as challenged to grow. The psychologist may recommend possible directions for further growth in your life such as a book to read, an issue to explore in spiritual direction or counseling, areas to pursue and develop in seminary or formation, or a 12-step program.

Use this professional as a resource for yourself. You may have questions about your emotional health, or your ways of coping or relating. This is an excellent opportunity to get suggestions for your personal growth and development.

Ask for clarity about who sees the report. Your vocation director may ask you to sign release forms during the application process because an admissions team or provincial council may decide who is to be admitted. It is appropriate for you to know who sees what is in the documents and reports gathered in your application process.

Remember to keep an honest and cooperative attitude during the process. Psychological testing picks up defensiveness or efforts to deceive. It is hoped that candidates for priesthood and religious life are growing in the virtues of honesty, humility and cooperation.

Chapter eleven

ACCEPTING "NO"

The most difficult part of the vocation director's job is telling an applicant that he or she will not be accepted. How to inform the person is handled differently according to the custom of the religious order or diocese.

Why would a diocese or community *not* accept someone who began the process of discernment with them? Here are some possible reasons:

1. The candidate was dishonest or failed to disclose something significant about his or her life.

2. As the full personality history is disclosed, the community cannot see the candidate living a happy, fulfilled life, given the community's particular charism and spirituality; or the diocese cannot envision the man living a happy, fulfilled life in the lifestyle and ministry of a parish priest.

3. Some basic skills are missing that need to be in place before a formation program begins; for example, the ability to pray and reflect on one's faith experience, social and communication skills, psycho-sexual maturity that is age appropriate, or autonomy skills.

4. Church law, called Canon Law, outlines some impediments for entry into a seminary or religious commu-

155

nity (Code of Canon Law, canon #1041). All of these impediments are open to canonical interpretation and possible dispensation. Don't assume you are excluded automatically because of one of these issues until you discuss it with the vocation director.

- A person who is suffering from insanity or psychic disorders judged by experts to make him unfit for orders.

- Apostasy, schism or heresy.

- A person who has attempted marriage, sacred orders, or a public vow to chastity while he/she was already married.

- A person who voluntarily murdered, aborted, or participated in an abortion.

- A person who has seriously and maliciously mutilated himself or others, or has attempted suicide.

- A person who has simulated the actions of a priest or a bishop.

5. Poor psychological report and negative letters of recommendation from former seminary or community.

Some communities will politely inform a candidate that she or he is too old, or that they are not "cut out" for their particular community or charism. Some vocation directors will say nothing.

Hearing "no" is a problem for some people. If a candidate has applied to several different communities or dioceses, and is not accepted, I suggest that she or he take a step back and listen to all the feedback from vocation directors.

ACCEPTING NO

Is there an obsession with a particular vocation? Do you only have a single issue that you talk about all the time? Is there an inability to get along with people? Poor social skills? Are you a non-stop talker?

If I *have* to be a priest, brother or sister in order to be happy, and I keep applying unsuccessfully, I need to reflect on the larger picture of my life. God speaks through all the circumstances, people and events of my life. What is this telling me? Part of the discernment of call is *confirmation* (see Chapter 3) in which I am accepted by a community or diocese of formation.

Ask your real friends, "What is there about me that might be difficult for a community?"

Having a mentor or spiritual director to debrief with after you've heard "no" is essential. You need someone with whom to talk over your feelings of anger, rejection, and disappointment.

If a community does not accept you, does it mean that you are not called to be a disciple of Jesus? No. Does it mean you are not called to holiness? Does it mean that you are not as good a person as another candidate who did get accepted? Does it mean that the community or vocation director just doesn't understand you? The answer to these questions is "No."

Canonically and theologically, no one has a *right* to priesthood or to religious life. It is not a right to be claimed. The call:

- Comes from a community (most likely your parish)

- Must be acknowledged and affirmed by others who know you well

VOCATIONS ANONYMOUS

- Must be recognized by the community or diocese that accepts you (This is the confirmation of the discernment)

I encourage people to ask vocation directors for honest feedback about the reasons for non-acceptance. Do not ask unless you genuinely want to hear what may be difficult to accept.

If you are not accepted by a particular community or diocese does it mean you are not called to the priesthood or religious life at all? No, not necessarily. But before you begin exploring elsewhere, take some time out to reflect on the experience, to pray for the faith to see the whole picture of your life. Go back to the basics of your life, remembering that God loves you and delights in you. Your baptismal call is your deepest, most profound call.

After some time to reflect, if you feel drawn and called to explore another community, pursue the process with them. I know of some people who began a process with one community, were not accepted, and are now happily living in another religious community.

I also know of some men and women who are extremely persistent and apply to place after place. It becomes violent to oneself to continue to pursue a vocation in which one is repeatedly not accepted. The cycle of hope and disappointment leads to unnecessary suffering. Listen to what God is saying through each part of the discernment and application process you have experienced.

In the inner freedom from your own agenda, strive to be open to whatever God reveals through the circumstances and events of your life. God's will is our peace.

158

PART IV
SPECIFICS

This section of the book examines some specific issues, struggles and concerns of those discerning a vocation. It offers practical suggestions and ends with my story, which I pray brings you some hope that there is light at the end of the discernment tunnel!

VOCATIONS ANONYMOUS

Chapter twelve

IT'S ALL IN THE TIMING

- When should I tell my family? My friends?

- How long should I wait to tell my boss?

- When do I need to refinance? Sell my house?

Every person has a different story and timeline. Given your own situation and circumstances, you will need to make timely decisions. Here are a few suggestions to help you.

At the beginning stages of discernment, when you are not sure about entering, I suggest that you do not tell your friends and family. This disclosure could change your relationships, leave you un-free, and add pressure to your decisions. People may begin to treat you differently. Friends may imagine you as "Father so and so" or "Sister Mary ____" and place unrealistic expectations on you. Some initial teasing could embarrass you. Questions may be invasive and interfere with your own process. Share your discernment with a spiritual director, vocation director, pastor or religious where respect, privacy, and your freedom will be held sacred.

When Is It Time To Phone The Vocation Director?

If you have a recurring thought to consider priesthood

or religious life, then it is time to make a phone call or speak to your pastor. Make an appointment with a vocation director. You are under no obligation to apply or to have clarity about your future when you meet with the vocation director. It is time to ask questions and to get some information about seminary and formation programs, charisms, and religious orders as well as the prerequisites for acceptance. It is time to learn what programs, retreats, and resources are available to help you with your discernment.

The time is yours to pray, reflect, and explore possibilities. I have known people who discerned and applied within three months; others discerned for a few years. The time is yours. Use it to get information, listen and pay attention to where God is leading. During this time you may want to ask a trusted friend or relative for feedback. This period of time gives you the opportunity to work on some prerequisites (paying off debts and student loans, living chastely, and experiencing ministry or service.)

If you have a romantic relationship with anyone with the possibility of a commitment, it will be difficult to seriously discern at the same time. I suggest that you discontinue a relationship that has this direction while discerning. Continue intimate, intentionally celibate relationships for support, growth and encouragement during this time.

When Is It Time To Apply?

Will Rodgers said, "I never made a mistake partly because I never made a decision!"

Don't wait until you are 100% certain! If you have visited the seminary or religious community, and feel pretty much at home there; if your head, heart and gut feel good about pursuing a future there, and if the receiving diocese or order welcomes and encourages you, then…*go for it!*

There will always be a few nagging doubts and questions. Ask for the application form and list of all the required documents.

When Should I Tell My Family and Friends?

Some people tell their family and closest friends when applying; others wait until they have been accepted. If they are not accepted, they are spared the task of explaining it all. Others want the support and feedback from other people. That choice is up to you, and depends on your relationships and situation.

When Should I Give Notice at Work?

It may be best to wait until you have a letter of acceptance from the seminary or religious order. If you have a job that offers a leave of absence, such as education or police work, you may take a leave. If you later discover that religious life was not for you, there's a job waiting. Some communities require a letter from your employer. Exceptions can be made to postpone such a letter so as not to unnecessarily jeopardize your job. Some religious communities want you to continue your present job during the first year of candidacy in the community. In that case, you don't give any notice.

When Should I Sell All I Have and Give Away My Belongings?

A man studying for the diocesan priesthood is able to keep his car, possessions, bank account, and other assets.

Each religious order has its own financial understanding with the candidates, postulants and novices. Most formation programs leave the candidate financially independent and responsible during initial formation.

It is *not recommended* for a person to get rid of all personal belongings at the time of entering a formation program. If you or the community decide after one month, six months or a year that religious life is not for you, there will be something to "go home to."

If you own your own home, you may want to refinance it, rent it out, or make some temporary arrangements rather than selling it, particularly if you are studying for the diocesan priesthood.

Once you have been accepted and have peace about your decision, it's party time! Begin the process of transition with some closure with your parish, friends and family. Celebrate the end of this stage of the discernment process and your new beginnings.

Chapter thirteen

WHAT HAS MY CULTURE GOT TO DO WITH IT?

Tina Turner sings, "What's love got to do with it?" The way we love is often influenced by our culture. The way we pray is also formed and shaped by our culture. "There is not one aspect of human life that is not touched and altered by culture."[53]

We are introduced to God and Church through the earliest experiences of our lives. Even if we do not remember certain events, they can still influence our choices and style of being in the world. Our homes and family shape our youngest selves. Young children believe what they are told and taught. As adults, we are able to take responsibility for what we choose and believe. In spite of this adult responsibility, we don't want to underestimate the influence our culture has had upon us.

Each family exists within a culture. Culture is difficult to define. It is almost impossible to explain a specific culture in terms of its value system, beliefs, and customs. "Each culture has its own characteristic manner of locomotion, sitting, standing, reclining and gesturing."[54] Within the US there are a multiplicity of cultures. Within the Archdiocese of Los Angeles, for example, there are 96 different Catholic

---

[53] Hall, Edward T. *Beyond Culture.* Garden City, NY: Anchor Press 1976, p. 16.
[54] *Ibid.* p. 75.

ethnic groups. Sunday Mass is celebrated in 42 languages! Each culture is a gift to the local church. Los Angeles is reportedly the most culturally diverse city in the world.

What has culture got to do with it? If you are called from a culturally diverse diocese to serve people, then part of your discernment is the gift and openness to minister to people of varying backgrounds.

If you are considering diocesan priesthood, find out what serving the people of your particular diocese entails. In Los Angeles, for example, no man is ordained unless he is bilingual (English and a second language for ministry). If you are considering an intentional religious community, you may end up living with community members of different cultures or living in other places in the world.

In discernment, consider your openness to other people who may have different ways of living, relating, and working. On a scale of 1 to 10, how flexible and adaptable are you? If you ministered to a person in another culture, could you adapt your words, gestures, and a way of proceeding to make the gospel message heard? Can you change your customs in order to make another person feel more comfortable? Are you familiar with your own prejudices and stereotypes? How stuck are you in your own way of doing things?

One of the stereotypes of US citizens abroad is that of being loud and confident people who assume that their way is the *best*, the most pragmatic, efficient, fast, and productive way! Other cultures challenge us to take time to *be*, to consider harmony in relationships before money; to respect the aged, and to be aware of nonmaterial realities. Since the US is so massive and powerful, we can be infected with some of the above assumptions.

To minister well is to reach people where they are, to preach the gospel in a way that it will be heard. We face a shadow of the challenge Jesus embraced when he let go of all when he became flesh through the Incarnation. Jesus' life as a human being, within a specific culture, time and place, is a model for us of that *kenosis*, that self-emptying and letting go.

Who, though he was in the form of God,
did not regard equality with God something to be grasped.
Rather, he emptied himself,
taking the form of a slave,
coming in human likeness;
and found human in appearance...

(Philippians 2: 6 – 7) Revised NAB

Jesus became flesh in a very specific culture – a culture with particular customs, traditions, ways of celebrating, marrying and praying. Jesus was conditioned to act and think within the culture that was his. Jesus was challenged to grow in age, grace and wisdom (cf. Luke 2: 52) as he moved beyond some of the Jewish cultural ways of thinking and behaving. The Syro-Phoenician woman, in begging Jesus to heal her daughter, challenged him by saying: "Please, Lord, even the dogs under the table eat the family's leavings" (Mark 7: 28). Jesus gradually expanded his sense of mission beyond that of the Jewish people. He was open to this Gentile woman's request. Perhaps he listened and reflected on her challenge and this enabled him to move beyond his culture. In Jewish culture, a man would not speak to a strange woman, particularly not a Gentile woman. Remember how shocked the disciples were when they discovered Jesus engrossed in a long conversation with a Samaritan woman at the well? (cf. John 4: 4 – 32)

Meditating upon the life of Jesus and his growth in age,

VOCATIONS ANONYMOUS

grace and wisdom can challenge us to continual conversion and growth. With regards to culture, we have many opportunities to grow in respect for the different customs of people without comparing or judging them against our own native culture. Language is sometimes a key to the difference in perception and values. For example, consider these different perceptions of time. In English, we speak of time "running out," or say, our watch is "running" well. Some other cultures say that "time walks." The Inuit are said to have forty different words for snow. We might be overawed at this, and yet we have more than forty different names for cars!

Family customs and responsibilities are unique to each culture. In many Vietnamese and Filipino families, the older siblings help pay for the education of the younger ones. As an older sibling does this for a few years, the next one in line accepts the responsibility. In Hispanic families, young people often give some of their salary to their parents. In some African cultures, a value is placed on the community and an effort not to stand out among one's peers. In some American families the value is on success and getting ahead!

Religious life has its own culture. It requires adaptation, even if you are entering into a homogenous situation. It may not be explained as explicitly as an ethnic culture, but it definitely has its own value system, customs, and identity distinct from any other culture. This may be what has been referred to as "unconscious culture." "Every culture has its own hidden, unique form of unconscious culture."[55]

You will want to explore how the diocese or community accepts a person from your culture. Are allowances made for the way your family may need to relate to you? Does the

---

[55] *Ibid.* Hall, p. 2.

168

WHAT HAS MY CULTURE GOT TO DO WITH IT?

worship experience of the diocese or community reverence different cultural expressions? If you are coming from and entering into a homogenous situation, this is not always a concern. There are very few of these homogenous situations left in the US, yet sometimes our cultural values can militate against the vowed life. Which of your cultural values could enhance religious life?

The cultural diversity of the Church and U.S. society presents significant challenges for individuals in vocation discernment. It requires consideration of your willingness to learn about other cultures, and to adapt for future ministry in a culturally diverse Church. It also challenges you to learn more about your culture of origin, to value your own ethnicity, to appreciate its impact on your self-identity, and to consider how this impacts your discernment and formation processes.

Do you know and treasure your own cultural roots? Where do your family traditions and values stem from? Since culture has great influence on how you think, work, value and relate, it would be important to be in touch with your own culture. This is not to be taken for granted. Some people are reluctant to claim their culture or origin. Some immigrant families have insisted on using only English in the home and have forgotten their native tongue. Not only does their cultural language get forgotten, but the values behind the customs, practices and beliefs are lost as well.

If I have not accepted and integrated my culture of origin, then it may show itself in different ways. One symptom of this lack of integration is denial. For example, someone from a Hispanic culture might refuse to learn Spanish for pastoral ministry. I have encountered some first and second generation candidates in denial about their culture of origin. A resistance to one's own background can be an ob-

169

stacle to self-knowledge and development. A second generation person may react to a situation without understanding
underlying cultural values of her first culture. For example,
she may hear selectively, or offend another person without
intending to do so. If certain topics are not discussed in my
family because of our culture, I may feel discomfort when
these issues are raised in conversation. Rules for courtesy
are different from culture to culture.

Similarly, if my culture is so much in the forefront of everything I do, so much so that I have no room for other
cultural expressions, this can also be a sign that I have not
integrated my culture well. This is manifested if I am not
inclusive in my world view, or if I politicize every comment,
observation, and action in order to put my culture first.

Poorly integrated cultural identity can also lead to carrying out traditional practices without an awareness of
their meaning. The discernment process can also be used
as a time to grow in self-identity, to learn your traditions
and to cherish the values of your culture of origin. Perhaps
some of your homework before entering will be to investi-
gate your own cultural background. Talk to your parents
and grandparents about your cultural values and how they
are expressed. If you are uncomfortable, you might explore
some of the negative stereotypes or caricatures of someone
of your own ethnicity. Examine who you are and value that
as part of God's creation.

Having said all this about cultural differences, it is also
important to recognize our common reality as human be-
ings. Carl Rogers said, "What's most personal is universal."
Given the respect due each culture, we still have a common
identity and need to have a common mission in priesthood
or in a religious order.

A Vietnamese woman who entered a cloistered Carmelite convent told me that sometimes we can place too much emphasis on our cultural differences. This Carmelite sister spoke of the more basic, deep down issues of the heart common to all. She quoted G. K. Chesterton, "Things common to all are more important than those peculiar to any one."[56] This reminder is important as we work towards unity and respect for all. We need to experience a unity beyond cultural differences.

---

[56] *Orthodoxy.* NY: John Lane Company, 1908.

VOCATIONS ANONYMOUS

Chapter fourteen

THE BABY ISSUE

One of the most profound losses a celibate experiences is the loss of having one's own child. This is even more difficult for cultures where family is the hope of the future and a way of living the afterlife.

My biological clock was ticking from age 37 to 40. I urgently wanted to have a baby and realized that the chances for that to happen were almost over. There was almost a sense of panic. I did not want to leave the convent. I was very happy as a religious, but I also knew I would make a good mother. In spite of all that, I felt a strong desire to be pregnant, to nurture and sustain life in my own womb; to feel its kick. I wanted to have my own child, to name it, hold it soon after birth, and watch it breathe on its own. I wondered what my baby would look like! (I did not have a father in mind.) Every baby I saw drew me in awe and amazement. I started to notice babies everywhere. I cried about this, prayed about it, and talked to a lot of friends.

It was painful for me to realize that I would never have my own child and that I would never be pregnant. This was not a surprise. When I took my vows in 1970, I realized that fact. Only years later did I *feel* the loss; it was a painful one. The pain was tangible as I walked through baby clothing sections in a store or held someone else's baby. The sisters I lived with suggested that I go to a home for pregnant girls

VOCATIONS ANONYMOUS

and hold some of the newborns. That didn't heal the loss of not being pregnant.

Over a couple of years I prayed about this desire and longing to have a baby. I talked to my spiritual director about it. I shared that desire with friends, family, and sisters in my community. Through the pain and loss, I discovered the beauty of a deeper challenge. I wanted to address this pain so that it would be life-giving, and so I would never grow bitter, cynical or hard.

I found some reflections and activities helpful and will share them here in case this is also your concern. Some of these reflections are very personal and may not resonate with your own experience. Monitoring my dreams, writing them down and working with them was also very revealing. I prayed for dreams that would help me process this desire to have a child and brought those dreams to spiritual direction. I found dream work very helpful.

My desire for pregnancy invited me to reflect on the annunciation and visitation in Luke's Gospel. I resisted "spiritualizing" this issue and desired to deal with it in a real human way – a woman's way. I also found consolation in meditating on these gospel passages.

"The Holy Spirit shall come upon you, and the power of the Most High will overshadow you…" (cf. Luke 1: 35)

This invitation to Mary inspired me to be more conscious of God's indwelling presence in my very body. Something is being done in me. I sensed a depth, a giftedness, a quiet growing deep down.

My spiritual director suggested that I read poetry of Angelus Silesius, from the 17th century. Here are some excerpts from his writings.[57]

---

[57] Franck, Francis, trans. *The Book of Angelus Silesius*. Santa Fe, NM: Bear and Co., 1976.

174

If by God's Holy Ghost thou are beguiled,
There will be born in thee the eternal child,
If it's like Mary, virginal and pure
Then God will impregnate your soul for sure.
God make me pregnant
And may this spirit shadow me
That God may rise up in my soul and shelter me
What good does Gabriel's "Ave Maria" do?
Unless he gives me that same greeting too?
I must be Mary and myself
Give birth to God
Would I possess
Nor can I otherwise
God's gift of everlasting happiness
If you hope to give birth to God on earth
Remember: God is not external
Conception takes place in the heart,
The womb of the Eternal.

During this time of reflection on pregnancy, I paid attention to women expecting a baby. I looked at a large photographic book with the themes of pregnancy and birth. I prayed with some of the most powerful photographs. I also physically and purposefully went into stores catering to pregnant women and mothers. I looked through the clothes and toys to put myself more in touch with the reality of pregnancy and birth.

What grew out of all of this was an awareness of another meaning of pregnancy. The conversion for me came in a reflection on pregnancy as I asked myself these questions:

- Do I allow the Spirit to overshadow me so that I too might bear the Word of God? So that God will take flesh in me?

- How attentive am I to my inner life? To giving each thing

time, not rushing growth. Mary kept all these things in her heart. How often do I ponder what God has done for me?

Conception, the first phase of this miracle, happens in darkness and quiet and often at an unknown time. Pregnancy cannot be rushed. It takes time; time to grow and develop. Only gradually is the mother aware of life within her. Her very own body and blood feeds this new life.

Birth happens through struggle, violence, pain and hard work. The baby travels from darkness and safety into light and noise. Consolation comes when the child is laid upon its mother's breast. The new baby is totally dependent. The parents are attentive at night sleeping with "one ear open." These realities also gave me an appreciation for all the mother goes through as well as what being a woman means at a deeper level.

In looking at all these phases, I prayerfully asked myself how I could develop these virtues as well. As a woman, I am called to develop the same gifts. How could I celebrate pregnancy? By being attentive to what is within, working hard to bring what is within to birth, and protecting what is most vulnerable. One of my reflections reads:

Let me thank God for this WOMB I have been given
For all its possibilities to bring forth
Let me look at it, feel its yearnings, and desire to nurture
Joyfully and thankfully.
After honestly realizing my possibilities
Let GOD draw me deeper into my own call to be celibate.
But celibate let me be, in a very warm, loving, vibrant way
Let me recall all the people – men, women and children
That I have loved and been loved by
Throughout the world

The intimate ways I have shared in their lives
Because for me celibacy has been life-giving!
The emptiness and the lonely moments have deepened in
me a compassion,
Have driven me into a deeper relationship with God.

Celibacy has been life-giving in that freedom to "carry" others within my heart and prayer for months. It has given me mobility for service, exposure and immersion into different cultures. It has driven me into prayer to search, work out, scrutinize, to roast on a fire, to be loved with an intensity I never thought possible by God who may at times be hidden, intangible, and even strange. The sexual tensions that have sometimes driven me up a wall, have also made grooves within me to be more life-giving, real, my words more credible, my ears freer to really hear the struggles of others. Some of that sexual energy has found life in music and creative surges I experience while jogging, praying and writing.

Archbishop Oscar Romero, who was assassinated in El Salvador in 1980, wrote, "God's eternal purpose has thought of all of you, and like Mary, he incarnates that thought in his womb." This stage of my life made me aware, not only of the *Indwelling Presence of God* in my very flesh, but also of my being in the "womb of God." I used this image in prayer, imagining myself as a fetus in the safe and nurturing womb of God.

After a few years of processing this loss, I no longer feel the pain. I have a deeper sense of the generativity of religious life and ministry. God has been faithful in the friends who companioned me through this stage of the journey.

If the issue of not having children and a family is crucial for you, talk to a priest or religious who has struggled with this issue themselves. Most candidates for priesthood or religious life are older now, and most likely already dealing with this midlife issue. Having a spiritual director enabled me to deal honestly and in a real way with the loss. It gave me compassion and appreciation for married women who long to have children and are not able to get pregnant. It gave me a deeper awareness of feminine gifts which could be used in ministry as well as in family life.

Chapter fifteen

DEVELOPING A HOLISTIC SPIRITUALITY

"The day of my spiritual awakening was the day I saw and knew I saw all things in God and God in all things," wrote Mechtild of Magdeburg. Do you recognize God in the kitchen? Do you experience God while you're exercising? Do you hear God in your car while driving? The mystic is the person who is aware of God's presence in everything and everywhere. To grow in prayer is to grow in sensitivity to this presence of God and in gratitude for the many gifts of God surrounding us. Those gifts are sometimes very earthy, sensuous, and what some label, "mundane."

One of the greatest obstacles to developing this all pervasive sense of God is the dualistic mindset that divides reality into the sacred and the secular. When we compartmentalize our lives into "spiritual" and "non-spiritual" activities, we can downplay God's presence and activity in what may be dismissed as "worldly." We have been influenced by *platonic disdain* for the body. This is why we read and hear about "saving our souls," referring to the immaterial part of ourselves. This dichotomy had such an effect on peoples' spirituality in the Middle Ages that married people who had intercourse thought it would be better not to receive the Eucharist; women had to be purified after giving birth; and women's bodies were thought to defile the sanctuary.

Holistic spirituality is a return to the Hebrew awareness of God-alive in every event. Their faith view looked at the totality. Each event of nature was interpreted in the light of faith. The body was not viewed in opposition to the spirit or soul; the body expressed faith. David danced naked before the Ark of the Covenant. The same Hebrew word used for making love also is used to describe loving God. This spirituality enables us to interpret our deepest human experiences as spiritual or sacred. Having a good glass of wine and listening to music could be a "spiritual" experience. "Like a seal of carnelian in a setting of gold is a concert when wine is served. Like a gold mounting with an emerald sea is string music with delicious wine" (Sirach 31: 27 – 28).

An African catechism answer to the question: "Why did God make me?" is "because he thought I'd like it." Creation reveals God's glory and presence, not only in nature, but in people; in our flesh and blood. African dances, drumming and celebrations deepen this sense of God's glory in creation and in the variety of cultures that God created.

The word *holistic* comes from the Greek word *holos*, meaning *whole.* Other derivatives of this word include healthy, whole, heal, hallow, and integral. A South African biologist, Jan Christian Smuts, introduced the concept that an organism cannot be understood by an analysis of its parts, but that it must be observed as a whole. This means observing it in its environment. The raw material for spiritual direction is not only your prayer practices, but the events, relationships, work and play which give context to your prayer. Holistic spirituality looks at the totality of your human experience in relation to God.

Jesus comes to meet us where we are. Jesus took on our flesh, walked this earth and made it holy. Our flesh and earth have been blessed by the Incarnation and Redemption.

DEVELOPING A HOLISTIC SPIRITUALITY

There is a deep down goodness about our bodies, physical sensations, emotions, art, music, and beauty. Jesus has blessed created reality by assuming our flesh and living in our world. All of these experiences have potential to draw us into God. I wonder if this is God's conspiracy – to seduce us into Love through the many gifts surrounding us!

The invitation in spirituality is to learn to recognize these gifts and integrate them into our relationship with God. Jesus grew in sensitivity to these gifts as he praised his Father while observing the birds of the air and the flowers of the field. Jesus prayed that his joy would be ours and our joy would be complete (cf. John 15: 11). He also said, "I have come that you may have life and have it to the full" (John 10: 10). Somewhere in the Talmud it says that when we die and come to judgment we will be held accountable for every legitimate pleasure that we *did not* enjoy.

This is quite a contrast from some old spiritual texts influenced by Pelagianism, which taught that we earned God's love and merited grace. Scripture teaches us that God has first loved us (cf. 1 John 4: 10). We are not good because we love God; we are good because God loves us. Spirituality influenced by the dichotomy between the sacred and the secular would have us believe that what is harder is holier; that physical penance inflicted on the body always earns us grace, that denying feelings and not entering into affectionate bonds with people will keep us freer for union with God. Rather than run away from these things, we may find God by entering into and going through experiences. The bottom line is that we do not earn God's love. We cannot become holy by our efforts. We are transformed by God's love and by trust in that love.

"Becoming holy, spiritual, is not nearly so much a question of running up a steep hill, carrying heavy weights and

181

VOCATIONS ANONYMOUS

puffing deeply, as it is a letting go of weights, letting go of the climb, and falling backward in trust, believing that we will be caught up in loving protective arms. It is not trying harder, but letting go."[58]

Have you experienced God in your body while dancing, running, swimming, preparing a meal, composing, playing music or singing, bathing, showering, receiving or giving a massage, or in any other sensual way? "All the glory of a mountain sunrise and much, much more is contained in your body sensations" (Tony de Mello, SJ).[59]

Brother Lawrence experienced God in the kitchen.

I possess God as tranquility in the bustle of my kitchen… as if I were on my knees before the Blessed Sacrament…it is not necessary to have great things to do. I turn my little omelet in the pan for the love of God…When I cannot do anything else, it is enough for me…When I cannot do anything else, it is enough for me to have lifted a straw from the earth for the love of God.[60]

The Practice of the Presence of God

The Jesuits have a focus in their spirituality of finding God in all things. It is a challenge to all of us to find God in the very "stuff" of our lives. This is holistic spirituality. A cultivation of this type of spirituality will better equip you to cope with the incredible changes that lie ahead in our society, church and religious life. An ability to find God in all things will give you proactive ways to deal with change no matter what lies ahead. Entrenchment in a spirituality that

---

[58] Dyckman, Katherine Marie, and Carroll, Patrick. *Inviting the Mystic, Supporting the Prophet.* Mahwah, NJ: Paulist Press, 1981.

[59] *Sadhana.* St. Louis: The Institute of Jesuit Sources, 1978, p. 17.

[60] Brother Lawrence of the Resurrection. *The Practice of the Presence of God.* Westwood, NY: Revell, 1958, pp. 28 – 29, 34 – 35.

creates a dichotomy between body and spirit can lead to a divided self. This is not holistic, or healthy.

Practical Suggestions for Living Holistic Spirituality

- *Live in the Present Moment.* This is not easy if you are the type of person tempted to worry about the future or hang on to the past. In our fast-paced society, it is difficult to stay in the here and now. Do what you are doing and be present to it. If you are drying dishes, be present to that moment. If you are praying, focus on your prayer, rather than giving in to distractions.

  "Trust the past to the mercy of God, the present to his love, and the future to his providence." – St. Augustine

- *Savor.* "Taste" your experiences. Reflect on them later or take time to "digest" them. We are so rushed that we often do not sit down for a meal but eat it on the run. We let the most precious moments escape without savoring them. (Meeting a friend, receiving a sacrament, recalling a significant memory.)

  "The true contemplative will teach us the art of savoring. If we savored more, we would buy less. We would be less compulsive, less unsatisfied. We would also work less and play more…if we savored more, we would communicate more deeply, relate more fully, compete less regularly and celebrate more authentically. We would be relating more deeply to ourselves, to creation in all its blessedness, to history past and future, to the now and to God."[61]

  When I taught first grade, a student brought me a gift one day. She had it all wrapped up in a small jewelry

---

[61] Fox, Matthew. *Original Blessing.* Santa Fe. MN: Bear & Co., 1983.

box. I spent some time undoing this gift because I could see how excited she was. After removing the ribbon, wrapping paper and the box top, under the cotton I discovered one big, ripe, juicy strawberry! This first grader could delight and savor the beauty of this strawberry. In her mind, it was a precious jewel and she wanted to share it with me.

- *Cultivate Daily Rituals.* There are daily activities that are opportunities for prayer. Every time I drive into the center of Los Angeles and see the high rise buildings, I pray for this city. You can designate "prayer triggers" for yourself. Perhaps these can occur while shaving, making your bed, watching the sunset or engaging in other daily activities.

Create your own rituals. Collect symbols that are important to you. Design your own prayer ritual. Perhaps you want to begin a new season in your life, acknowledge a loss or transition, or symbolize a phase of the discernment journey. Candles, music, incense, oil, chimes, holy water, cards, statues, sculptures, or icons could be part of it. It would be important to incorporate only those objects that have meaning for you personally. Use some actions in your ritual – a Sign of the Cross, or a blessing. Dance, sing a song, do whatever you need to do to make your prayer meaningful.

You might want to create a prayer corner in your room or a sacred space in your home. I always keep a small ritual bag in the trunk of my car or in my suitcase when I travel. It contains a small Mexican cloth, candle, small New Testament and Psalms, and an icon. Wherever I am, I can create a prayer space, away from home and chapel, by setting up these things on the prayer cloth.

- *Intend to give the ordinary meaning.* You can enhance the ordinary by giving it a meaning. For example, as I wash my car I can intend that my efforts will heal my temper. As I take a shower, I can be intentionally grateful for the gift of water which purifies, heals and invigorates. Looking in the mirror can be a reminder that we were created by love and for love. Gardening can be an opportunity to work with the Creator God. As a Bemba proverb says, "To dig a root is to mix with God." As we get our hands in the dirt, we can recall the Creator God who breathed into the clay in Genesis.

  As part of your morning prayer, visualize the day before you. Who will you meet? What will you be doing? Imagine the light of God, the loving presence of God penetrating and enlivening the details of your day.

  At night, as part of your prayer, quickly review the day. Where did you miss out on what was happening in the moment? What do you want to savor? Where was God present? Where could you have been more loving?

- *Cultivate beauty in your life.* "This soul can be poisoned through the ear" writes Thomas Moore in *Care of the Soul*.[62] Make sure that some form of beauty – art, music, poetry, literature – is an integral part of your life and discover God in that beauty. Enjoying nature is another powerful vehicle for God's grace. One of the most profound prayer experiences of my life was standing in a grove of Redwood trees in northern California. I was overcome, overwhelmed and could not speak. Fortunately, I had the space, solitude, and time to absorb some of this experience of God's presence. St. John of the Cross used these images of nature to describe his union with God.

---

[62] New York: Harper Perennial, Harper Collins, 1992.

VOCATIONS ANONYMOUS

> *"My beloved is the mountains, and lonely wooded*
> *valleys, Strange islands, and resounding rivers,*
> *The whistling of love-stirring breezes,*
> *The tranquil night*
> *At the time of rising dawn,*
> *Silent Music*
> *Sounding solitude,*
> *The supper that refreshes and deepens love."*

- *Reflect.* Don't let life pass you by. Reflection enables us to see God at work where we may have been too busy to notice. God is in our human experience. "We receive God in experience. We do not project, create, or posit God in experience. Rather, we find God, already here, ahead of us, in human experience."[63] Journaling is a way for some people to reflect and remember graced moments. This reflection helps us to be grateful. Whether we remember pain or joy, grace or sin, the important thing is for us to pay attention, to notice. In order to develop a holistic spirituality, you need to reflect on how you encounter God in your relationships, in your body and at work, as well as in other more obvious moments, such as in the sacraments, nature, or your prayer time.

Reflection will enable you to work towards a holistic stance that discovers God in any area of life. If you catch yourself downplaying your physical, sexual, relational or emotional experiences, or detaching them from your spiritual life, stop and see if you can invite these experiences into your prayer. Is there a dichotomy there? A split self? If you have difficulty facing and acknowledging some of these experiences, then all the more reason to reflect on them.

Learning to embrace and incorporate everything into

---

[63] Lane, Dermot. *The Experience of God. An Invitation to do Theology.* NY: Paulist Press, 1981.

your relationship with God leads to a healthy, whole-some, genuine union with God. Keeping your "spiritu-al" life separate from all the rest of the "worldly" areas of life, will keep you from integrating all that happens and be an obstacle to finding God in all things. This analogy of prosthesis by Mark Link, SJ, describes the difference between holistic and dualistic spirituality. "For some people, religion is like an artificial limb. It has neither warmth nor life, and although it helps them to stum-ble along, it never becomes a part of them. It must be strapped on each day."

Self Test for Holistic Attitudes

1. Where in your daily routine do you meet God (apart from prayer)?

2. Is there any area of your life that you do not bring into your prayer conversation with God? Why don't you?

3. Apart from church and sacraments, where do you most vividly experience God?

4. Where do you most vividly encounter peace, wholeness, and connectedness with life? Is God an integral part of your awareness in this experience?

5. Into what area of your life could you more consciously invite God?

6. Name a relationship in which you have experienced God.

7. Name a physical sensation or gesture that has become holy (whole) for you.

8. Is God part of your play life, and not just your prayer life? How?

VOCATIONS ANONYMOUS

Chapter sixteen

BEING A WOMAN IN THE CHURCH

The question I have heard often is, "How could a woman enter religious life in the church today when she is not allowed full participation in church leadership and ministry?" Men have been asking questions too about women's participation in church decision making. This is a problem some of the women discerning religious life face. Over the years, several other women came into the vocation office saying that they felt called to priesthood and wondered what their response should be. One of those women went to study at Harvard; a few others worked on their Masters of Divinity degree in hopes that there would be more choices available to them in the future. This is an issue that will not go away. It may well resemble the evolution of consciousness that led the Church to change its stance on slavery, indulgences, limbo, who could be in the sanctuary and who could distribute Eucharist. Theologians, scripture scholars and church historians continue to study and revisit the role of women from early Church as well as looking at Jesus' inclusion of women in his ministry. None of this should stop a woman from saying "Yes" to the call she senses from God by further studies, using her voice, entering a religious community and accompanying the people of God on this issue.

How does a woman deal with this question and with all the subsequent questions that emerge over this issue? One way of coping is to become educated about the issue. We have a heritage, a family tree as women in our church that we can be proud of and that we haven't heard much about. So stand back and look at the issue in its historical context. As you learn more about Church history and theology, particularly the stories that have *not* been told, you may experience some anger. Women functioned in the church more fully in ages past. We know from New Testament studies that the Christian community met in households of women and that women gathered the community for Eucharist. There have been women who advised the Pope, reformed orders, and served the poor when there were no social programs. There is a history that women need to reclaim. It is a history of speaking out, reforming, creating new models of ministry, and risking being on the cutting edge.

Another way of coping is to bring any frustration, anger or disappointment to prayer. My image of God has changed over the years as I have wrestled with being a woman in the church. I sometimes envisage God as my coach, putting me in predicaments and places where women are not often found. My feminine images of God have grown stronger and compliment the masculine images that nurtured me for years. My sense of God has expanded and deepened as I discover in God what is most feminine. When I took a feminist theology course, the unexpected happened. I braced myself for the inevitable anger I knew would result from being better informed. I enjoyed the reading required for the class. The unexpected growth was that I grew more in love with Jesus, and read the Gospel differently. I encountered a Jesus who was challenged to expand his mission not only to the Jews, but also to the Gentiles through the encouragement of the Syro-Phoenician woman. Jesus angered the religious authorities and scandalized his own disciples by his openness to women and how he encouraged them. He allowed

Mary to sit at his feet, the traditional posture of a disciple being trained by a rabbi.

I also needed to view the changes that have taken place during my lifetime in order to glean some hope from these developments. When I entered the convent, I imagined the most I would ever do was teach religion in an elementary school or in a religious education program. Religious education is a precious gift and most of the catechists are women. It is, however, only one of many ways women can serve the church and preach the Gospel.

In the years since the Second Vatican Council more opportunities for leadership in the Church have opened for women. Women read at liturgy, distribute the Eucharist, and in some circumstances, preach. In Zambia, I was asked to lead communion services and to preach when there were no priests. Gradually, my ministry expanded to include vocation work for both men and women, previously reserved for priests.

I need to remind myself at times of the evolution and development of women's participation and role in the Church. The difficulty for me is in balancing appropriate patience with the wisdom to know when to speak up and raise more consciousness of this issue.

In summary, women trying to cope in the Church can:

1. Get educated. Know the facts so you can present the case for women by being well-informed.

2. Incorporate this desire for justice and your feelings about the lack of justice into your prayer life.

3. Keep the present in perspective, acknowledging that there is movement forward.

4. Honor a balance between speaking out when appropri-
    ate, and raising the consciousness in others while not
    alienating those who may not be as conscious of the is-
    sues, men and women alike.

When in confusion, I focus on Jesus. What would he
have said? What would he have done? How would he have
treated women in this case? The gospel is my grounding
rather than any historical basis in an argument.

Some Women Pioneers

Some of the great women of our Church have been an
inspiration and encouragement to me. Here is a brief listing and biographical sketch. You might want to read more
about women who pique your interest. See if you can discover something in their lives that enabled them to go beyond the confines of any system.

Brigid of Kildare – In Ireland, Brigid was consecrated a
bishop instead of an abbess when Bishop Mel of Longford
read the wrong ritual. When it was pointed out to him, St.
Mel said, "It is the will of God; it shall stand." Brigid was
the founder of a powerful Christian community, 60 local
churches, and the leader of both the men's and women's
monasteries.[64]

St. Hildegaard of Bingen (great abbess of the Middle
Ages) – founded and governed great monasteries that were
centers of prayer, education, medicine, science, and the arts.
At one time excommunicated, she is now a canonically recognized saint.

St. Catherine of Siena – Doctor of the Church, a third
order Dominican who advised the Pope to return to Rome

---

[64] Sellner, Edward C. *Wisdom of the Celtic Saints.* Notre Dame, IN: Ave Maria
Press. 1993, pp. 70 – 71.

from Avignon and challenged other Bishops about their lifestyles; Catherine, a mystic, wrote her conversations with Jesus in *The Dialogue*, and lived with the stigmata.

St. Teresa of Avila – Doctor of the Church, a mystic and writer who, along with St. John of the Cross, reformed the Carmelites. In one of my favorite stories, it's said that Teresa danced on the table during recreation!

St. Bridget of Sweden – married with eight children, founded the Brigettine Order of Sisters; she later went to Rome and was the advisor to three popes!

St. Elizabeth Ann Seton – the first American born saint was the mother of five children, a widow and a convert to Catholicism. She founded the Sisters of Charity and died at the age of 46!

Sr. Thea Bowman – A Franciscan Sister, teacher, artist, gospel singer and evangelist who taught priests how to preach. The granddaughter of a slave, Thea earned her Ph.D. in English literature and linguistics.

Edwina Gateley – Founder of the Volunteer Missionary Movement which now has 400 missionaries all over the world. She also founded Chicago's Genesis House, which is a housing and rehabilitation program for sexually exploited women. Edwina is still a prophetic witness and an author of several books.

There are many, many more holy women who have responded to needs in our Church. Some of them will never be known or written about. These are just a few to spark your own imagination.

Do you have your own list?

VOCATIONS ANONYMOUS

Chapter seventeen

MY OWN VOCATION STORY

A lot more happens on the beaches and freeways of Southern California than you hear about on the news. Yes! God has actively moved and spoken in these places. I was brought up in a Catholic family and attended Catholic schools until my junior year of high school. I went along with Catholic formation, received Eucharist, was confirmed, played the organ in church, did not eat meat on Fridays and went to confession. But my first significant encounter with God happened quite by surprise during my junior year of high school.

My family was living in San Clemente at the beach, and I was attending San Clemente High. I went up to church to practice the organ for a wedding. It was an ordinary weekday and no one was around the church. As I walked down the aisle, I spied a book left behind in one of the benches. I picked it up and casually began reading, *The Presence of God*. As I read, I became very aware of God's presence in that church. I sat down in the pew instead of heading up to the choir loft, and was captivated in prayer for over an hour. For the first time in my life, I had an overpowering sense of the reality of God. God was real. God was present in the here and now in a way I had never before experienced.

It was not the kind of experience you rush home to discuss at the dinner table. I am the eldest of eight children and belong to quite an extroverted family. Secretly, I began to return to this experience and made clumsy efforts to begin praying. I read the book and then decided it was time to return it to the owner. When I asked at the rectory who the book might belong to, the priests informed me that a community of sisters had just moved into the parish, and that most likely one of them had left the book in the church. I drove up to the hill and knocked on the convent door. The sister who answered the door was very friendly and very relieved that her book had been found. I told this sister how much this book had affected me, and that it planted in me a strong desire to pray. This Sister, Una O'Neill, took me "under her wing" and coached me along the ways of prayer for the next year or so.

My vocation to religious life began with this desire to live a life of prayer. I was embarrassed to talk about it, especially since I was not the pious type. I kept it to myself and yet maintained a practice of at least an hour in quiet prayer each day. During my senior year, I explored a few communities, but really felt called to the community who I had met in San Clemente, the Religious Sisters of Charity. My mom was already suspicious. I asked my dad if he would come to see a novitiate one Sunday. He sat me down and grilled me on all the reasons I was not called to religious life. It turned out that he was really thrilled, but wanted to make sure I felt free and not pressured to do this.

I entered the convent in September 1967 with lots of fears and doubts. I went through postulancy and a two year novitiate wondering if I'd be thrown out. We were still living a pre-Vatican II form of religious life. My name was changed to Sr. Mary Joseph. I kept silence, prayed, cleaned house, played jokes on people, tried to diffuse my sexual energies, and took classes in philosophy, scripture and theology.

After I was professed, I taught elementary school for a few years and then went back to college to earn a BA. I majored in music (piano) at California State University at Long Beach. That must have been quite a sight – a blue veiled nun in the band room playing a trombone! I earned my teaching credentials, taught junior high, and then my life took a new direction.

The sisters asked me to go to Ireland, where our congregation began. I moved to Dublin and taught religion at a girls' high school. When priests would ask what I was doing in Ireland, I enjoyed telling them that I was a missionary. That got mixed reactions! Not too long after my arrival, I went to a Dominican priory for confession. The prior recommended that during my stay in Ireland, I go to confession and get spiritual direction from one of the priests living there named Fr. Anselm Moynihan, OP. A week later, I spied on this priest to see what he was like as he celebrated Sunday liturgy. I observed an older, quiet, holy looking, introverted priest. I also discovered that he was a scholar and wrote articles for a magazine. He didn't sound like the spiritual director for me, but something told me to trust the judgment of the prior. I went for it. Fr. Anselm was indeed a quiet, holy, and wise priest.

After a year in Ireland, I was eager to return home to California. My regional superior wrote and asked me to pray about my next ministry. I began listening and discerning where God might be calling me next. The scripture passage that grabbed me immediately was: "Leave your country and your father's house and go to the land I will show you."[65] I was so shocked that I closed the bible and only pretended to pray for the next two weeks. I went into the chapel with the other sisters, but avoided listening at all costs. I couldn't live

---

[65] Genesis 12:1

without truly praying since it was my lifeline, so I returned to listening to God. Still, I kept hearing the same invitation to move on. I figured that the other option was to go to Africa. But I was a piano major. I loved the beach. How could God ask a California beach girl to go to Africa? Not having been a girl scout, I didn't have any practice at outdoor skills!

I shared this repeated sense that I was to move on with my spiritual director. He told me that it was probably my imagination and not to volunteer. I didn't. But as the weeks passed, I noticed that my initial resistance to going to Africa subsided, and my heart did a 180 degree turn. Then the local superior called me in one night. Our superior general had just returned from Zambia. This sister asked me to pray about something and not to feel any pressure to respond immediately. She asked if I would think about going to Namwala, Zambia! It turns out that after saying "Yes" and going to Zambia, I had the five happiest years of my life!

Just before I left Ireland, I visited Sr. Una O'Neill whom I had met in San Clemente in the 60's. Sister Una reminded me of the book that had inspired me to pray, the book she had forgotten in the church. Una told me that the author lived in Dublin and that it would be nice to visit him and tell him that he planted a seed. I agreed and asked for his name. It turned out to be Fr. Anselm Moynihan! I ran down Dorset Street and into the priory in amazement to tell him of my discovery. I reminded him that I lived a small town called San Clemente in 1966 and that I read an important book. He was tickled when I told him that it was his book. In 1966, he was prior of San Clemente in Rome. Somehow God's providence had connected San Clemente, Rome, Dublin and Zambia in my life. This priest prayed for me every day at noon. I visited him and Sr. Una whenever I travelled to Ireland. It is only years after all this happened that I could see God's providence at work in it all. On the surface, all I experienced was finding a forgotten book, meeting a sister, and going to a quiet priest for spiritual direction. Upon reflection, I can see God's hand in all of it.

From the beach of San Clemente to the bush of Namwala, Zambia, I experienced the faithfulness of God. From being called Sr. Mary Joseph, back to Sr. Kathy and then to Sr. Choolwe Namoonga, I learned to be flexible! The Zambian people evangelized me, taught me what reverence for God means and shared a faith that sees God alive in all that happens. I could go on and on with wonderful stories of life in Zambia.

After teaching in a government school in Zambia and helping students prepare for the sacraments, I was asked to return to the U.S. On the way home, I studied spiritual direction and made a 30 day retreat at St. Beuno's, Wales. There was a wonderful group of priests, religious and lay people from India, South America, Thailand, Ireland, Britain, and Europe! We shared faith and practiced spiritual direction on each other!

When I returned to California, the sisters asked me to take some time to discern where God was calling me. Starting at square one again, I had no idea where to look. I explored campus ministry, pastoral ministry in a parish, high school, retreat work, and youth ministry. One day, a sister asked me to fill in for her and give a vocation talk. I gave the talk with several priests. One of the priests asked me if I'd be interested in vocation ministry. It turned out (Divine Providence struck again!!) that there was a job opening for a woman religious on the diocesan level. I went for interviews and was offered the ministry to help young adults discern their call. This job gave me the scope, creative possibilities, retreat work, spiritual direction, and opportunity to share my own vocation with people discerning their own call. After spending twenty-one years in the vocation office, I look back and appreciate how enriching that time was through sharing in the lives of those discerning their call to religious life and priesthood.

Through vocation ministry, I have ended up doing things I never expected to do: running marathons to promote Church vocations, giving retreats at seminaries, creating ministry immersion events for young adults, discernment groups, writing and speaking. The best part of the job was meeting wonderful people in discernment and getting glimpses of God at work in their lives.

Throughout my life as a woman religious, I have lived in a community of sisters. It is a wonderful thing to discover that you have a home and a group of people who accept you no matter where you go. I have stayed in our convents in Africa, California, England, Scotland, Venezuela, Ireland, and Australia. Even though I may not have known the sisters living in each convent, as soon as I walked in the door, I felt at home and welcomed.

We also have the luxury of living in a home or convent with a chapel. Prayer has continued to be the only way I can survive honestly in this lifestyle. It was the way God seduced me into the convent in the first place.

Ten things to do before you enter the convent, seminary or formation program:

1. *Look back at your history.* You made important decisions in the past. You made some good choices. How did you go about the good decisions? How did God lead you? How do you best hear God? Tune into that pattern.

2. *Do your emotional homework first.* Deal with unresolved anger, authority issues, sexual hang ups. Forgive those against whom you bear a grudge. Join a 12-step group for a while if you need to resolve codependency or addiction issues. Short term counseling may be helpful.

3. *Thank those significant people in your life that helped you to get to where you are now.*

4. *Pay attention to the spirits!* Notice how the Holy Spirit leads you into life-giving, energizing, hopeful dreams. Know yourself and your vulnerabilities to particular thoughts or movements that lead to depression, doubt or fear. Go with the good spirit.

5. *Use your imagination.* Do some "holy daydreaming." Imagine yourself doing some great things for God.

6. *Do some fun things you have always wanted to do as a child.* Try one thing you've been afraid to do! (Rollerblading, skiing, painting, playing an instrument.) Take a risk!

7. *Cultivate a sense of humor!* You'll need it in a formation program. Read the funny papers. Lighten up! Don't take yourself too seriously.

8. *Do something for your body.* Take a walk, stretch, swim, or get a massage.

9. *Get a support system in place* of people who will promise to pray for you, visit you, write letters or call.

10. *Party!* Celebrate with close friends your new beginnings. Perhaps you could create a prayer or ritual. Be creative.

VOCATIONS ANONYMOUS

PART V:
SPACE FOR PRAYER

VOCATIONS ANONYMOUS

PRAY CREATIVELY

There can be no genuine discernment without quality time for prayer. You can talk to as many people as you like, read books, and visit seminaries and communities. It will all be futile without listening to what God has to say. Prayer also affords us the time to listen to our deeper selves and to the desires of our hearts.

This section offers suggestions for prayer beyond the "saying" of set prayers. If you are just beginning to pray more deeply, you will find suggestions here that may help you. If you have had a healthy prayer life for some time, you may encounter some new ideas here for deepening your relationship with God.

Note that the section is divided into two parts. The first part describes methods of prayer, while the second offers some prayer exercises that you might try. Don't be fooled into thinking that as you read this section, or any book on prayer, you are actually praying. The temptation can be to vicariously live the experience of another person.

These suggestions are simply meant to get you started. To enter into the depth of self and encounter with God, requires the risk of coming to God without any defenses, such as books, exercises, or journals. These are meant as helpful guides only. If they lead you to a deeper relationship with God, their purpose has been accomplished. If you find them distracting, then abandon them for the type of prayer God calls you to in your heart.

205

VOCATIONS ANONYMOUS

METHODS FOR PRAYING

Prayer 101: Some Simple Ways to Pray for Beginners

Prayer is about growing a relationship with God. If you never have had any guidance for prayer, or if you are unsure about how to proceed, here are some simple ways to begin.

- Find a quiet place. Start with five minutes of listening, of just being present to God. Do this by imagining that you are sitting with an old friend. You may not have to say anything. Remember that you are in the presence of someone who loves you beyond anything you could ever realize or imagine.

- Make an appointment with God. Sometimes the best intentions never materialize because we get too busy or other things always seem to interfere. Write down the time and place in your calendar and honor the appointment as if you were with someone very important that you just had to meet!

- Just listen. If you have a difficult time settling down to pray, and you cannot imagine how this listening to God can take place, begin by listening to all the sounds you can hear outside the room or building. If you are outside, just pause and listen to all the sounds surrounding you. This can have a calming effect on a racing mind.

- These images, or others you think of, may also help you prepare for prayer. Be present to God:

VOCATIONS ANONYMOUS

– As if you are a child asleep on its mother's lap (Psalm 131)

– As if you are floating on your back in the ocean or a pool

– As if sitting with a loved one with whom no words are necessary

- Particularly if you are looking at the priesthood, you will want to deepen your sacramental prayer life. Attending daily liturgy is a tremendous blessing for those in discernment. Receiving the sacraments regularly is an area for you to work on if you are not already faithful to that part of your prayer life.

- Use music to encourage you, comfort, challenge, and help you to quiet down to be in God's company

More Suggestions for Prayer
(Beyond "saying prayers" for beginners)

1. Take a walk at a quiet time in a relatively quiet place. Turn off the iPod or cell phone. Listen instead through ears filled with sounds of God's creation…notice…pay attention. Don't think great thoughts or attempt to "figure anything out."

2. Cultivate a habit of "putting the day to rest" each night, a suggestion of Fr. Leo Rock, SJ. For ten to fifteen minutes, rewind and play back the images of the day. Review your day. Do you notice anything that you didn't pay much attention to at the time?

3. At the car wash, the bank, the store, the gym, or on the freeway onramp, take a personal inventory check. What

208

METHODS FOR PRAYING

do you notice there? Peace? Tugs and pulls? Unrest? It helps to have personalized prayer spaces. Where do you meet God? I find that the car is often the place where God speaks to me. In fact, I sense God as I drive on the freeways of Los Angeles! I have sensed God alive in my body while running, doing Zumba or working out. Get to know the places and spaces in your life where you can recognize the presence of God.

4. Take off your shoes before the burning bush as Moses did! (Exodus 3: 1 – 5) How? Turn off the radio or iPod in your car for a few minutes. Make the choice to turn it off and intentionally listen. Listening doesn't mean that you hear definite words or come up with a solution to a problem. It means a coming home to self. When you check-in often with your inner self, you will:

- Meet God there

- Know yourself better, be in better touch with yourself

5. Build into your life some signposts for prayer or "triggers" for prayer. Take some ritual that is part of your daily life and attach a prayer or an attitude to it. Each time I pass downtown Los Angeles on the Harbor Freeway, and see the high-rise buildings, I say a prayer for our city. When I make my bed in the morning, I remember that I am loved by God unconditionally. There are ways you can use shaving, showering, or looking in a mirror as triggers for prayer.

6. Take your Bible off the shelf or coffee table. Find a short passage, for example, Isaiah 43: 1. Read it slowly. Sit with the text. Don't analyze it. Imagine God speaking to you through the passage. Read it as if God is speaking to you personally.

209

VOCATIONS ANONYMOUS

"Fear not, (your name) , for I have redeemed you; I have called you by your name: you are mine."

When you pass through the water, I will be with you... because you are precious in my eyes, _____

Fear not, _____

Continue with the text. We believe that the Bible is God's word to us. It is a living word, not something written a long time ago for someone else. It is written for you, to be heard in the circumstances of your life today.

This simple method of prayer can be used with any scripture passage. Some other passages that you might select for starters:

Psalm 139	Psalm 103	John 14 & 15
Romans 8	Philippians 4	Luke 5: 1-15
Mark 4: 35 – 39	Luke 5	Jeremiah 29: 11-15
Proverbs 3: 3 – 61	Kings 19	Wisdom 9
Isaiah 61	Psalm 23	Luke 10: 38-42
Isaiah 49: 13 – 18	Jeremiah 1: 4-10	Luke 1: 26-38
Romans 12: 1 – 13	Ephesians 1: 3-12	Isaiah 55: 1-11

When It's Difficult to Pray

If you have difficulty getting quiet to pray, and are pestered by a lot of distracting thoughts, try using one of the following three ways to become still:

1. *Breathe* – Focus on your breathing for a few minutes before you read the scripture text. Center yourself in your body. Let go. Listen to yourself breathe in and out. Feel the breath as it enters your nostrils and goes down into

METHODS FOR PRAYING

your body. Let go of your anxieties, cares and concerns as you exhale.

2. *Listen* – If you are inside a room, listen to all the sounds outside. Listen to your heart. Is there something clamoring for attention? A need, a feeling unnoticed? An inner child? Spend time listening to all that surrounds you rather than fighting the sounds as "distractions."

3. *Focus* – Gaze upon an image that may help you center. Focus on something like the flame of a candle, a cross, an icon, a tree, the ocean. If not an image, focus on one word: Light, Jesus, or Peace. Whenever you find yourself distracted during the rest of your prayer time, come back to this visual or verbal focus.

The Five "P's" of Prayer

Fr. Armando Nigro, SJ, suggests that when we pray with scripture, we remember the five "P's":

• <u>Passage</u> from scripture. Have one picked out, marked and ready for prayer some time before you start.

• <u>Place</u>. Find a quiet place where you will be undisturbed. Plan ahead of time where you will pray.

• <u>Posture</u>. Make sure you are comfortable but not so comfortable that you'll fall asleep.

• <u>Presence</u> of God. Begin by remembering that you are in God's presence. When you drift away, peacefully return to this reality.

• <u>Passage</u>. Read the passage slowly. Sometimes it helps to read aloud. Sit with the passage. Listen. Stay relaxed.

Lectio Divina (Sacred Reading)

The Benedictine tradition practices a way of praying called *Lectio Divina*. The method leads one into a deeper encounter with the Word of God through participating in four steps.

- *Lectio* – Read the text with faith and openness.

- *Meditatio* – Meditate on what you read by pausing where something strikes you. Repeat a word or phrase that is meaningful for you. Ponder what you have read.

- *Oratio* – Pray in your own words. The text may stimulate some matters for your prayer.

- *Contemplatio* – Be present to God in a loving, attentive way. No words are necessary. Take "a long loving look at the Real."

There is no set amount of time to be spent in each of the four phases. Contemplation is a gift. Most days we might find ourselves doing *lectio, meditatio,* and *oratio,* and then heading out for the day. Welcome the gift if it comes. We cannot force contemplation or earn it by working for it.

Prayer in the Ignatian Tradition

The Ignatian tradition offers another method for praying with scripture. This method uses all of our senses and our imagination to immerse us in the scripture passage. St. Ignatius invites us, after reading the passage, to enter into the text by imagining ourselves as one of the characters in the story. Ignatian contemplation invites us to see through our own eyes the event as if we were watching it being filmed.

Ignatius says that we should see, hear, smell and touch

METHODS FOR PRAYING

each facet of the event. As we experience the gospel scene, we are called to be aware of how we respond on a feeling level and to consider what it might mean for us at this time. Ignatius suggests that we open the time of prayer with a request for a special grace that we articulate in our own words. He suggests that we close the time of prayer with gratitude, an offering of ourselves and the Lord's Prayer.

Try praying the way St. Ignatius suggests using the story of the healing of the man who had been sick for 38 years, from John 5: 1 – 16.

- Before prayer, choose a place and mark the passage.

- Make yourself comfortable and begin by remembering that you are in God's presence. Ask God, or better yet, beg God for a specific gift you need.

- Read the passage. Imagine the setting for this story as vividly and concretely as you can. What does the pool look like? What do you hear? How does it smell? Does anyone reach out to touch you? Look at the people. What kind of people are they? What are they doing?

- Insert yourself into the scene. What are you doing there? Why have you come? What are your feelings as you look over the place and watch the people? Notice the sick man who has been suffering for 38 years. What do you say to him? As you are speaking, Jesus approaches. What are his actions? How does Jesus act? What does he say? What does the man answer? (Sometimes in your prayer the story can change and take an unexpected twist. Allow this to happen. Often something very significant is revealed to us in these changes.) Listen to the dialogue between Jesus and the sick man. Notice the reactions of the man upon being healed.

213

VOCATIONS ANONYMOUS

- Jesus now turns to you. He engages you in conversation. Talk to him about the miracle. Is there any sickness that you suffer from? Any need for healing in your life? Speak to Jesus about it. Perhaps he asks, "Do you want to get well?" "Are you ready for all the consequences of a cure?"

- Listen to the words of Jesus as he prays for your healing or as he lays his hands on you. What are you feeling?

- Spend a while now in quiet prayer in the company of Jesus

- Give thanks and close with a prayer in which you offer yourself to God.

- Say the Lord's Prayer.

St. Ignatius recommends that after a period of prayer, the person spend some time reviewing and reflecting on how the prayer went. Was it alive? Dry? Was I too tired or distracted? What did I hear? What did I feel? (Peace, restlessness, joy, boredom, resistance) What do I want to remember?

Become familiar with the way that God speaks to you, or rather, the way you best hear God. Lovers relate very personally. The lover knows how to read the most subtle nuances of the loved one. Can you recognize the imprint of God's fingers in your day?

214

METHODS FOR PRAYING

Spiritual Exercises of St. Ignatius: Making Choices[66]

Here are a variety of different exercises proposed by Fr. Hewett, SJ.

1. Become still using breathing, focusing or body relaxation. Let the matter for choice arise. Imagine you are another person coming to ask the real, actual you about your problem. Listen while s/he speaks. How does it feel? What has become clearer?

2. Let the matter for choice arise. Imagine that you are on your deathbed. Not very much longer to go. You are very lucid and you look back. What will you wish you had done? Jesus visits you. He looks; he listens; he smiles. What do you say?

3. Let the matter for choice arise. What does the child in you say? What does the young person say? The middle age person in you? The old wise person?

4. Let the matter arise. Is there play or creativeness in it? Is it merely frivolous? Is there risk or adventure in it? Is it merely foolhardy? Is there depth or compassion in it? Is it merely hard? Is there wisdom or fulfillment in it? Is it merely a whim?

5. Let the matter arise. Be aware; deliberately discount and drop what friends or admirers, however good, say. Let drop what enemies say. Let drop, discount whatever book you've read. Discount what thinking, however logical and straight. Let drop, discount, what your feelings, either way, are saying. Now…what do you really want?

6. Let the matter arise. Let all the pros arise. Reasons, feel-

---

[66] Used with permission from Fr. William Hewett, SJ.

VOCATIONS ANONYMOUS

ings, images…How does it feel? Now go away and think about or do something totally different for at least an hour…perhaps a day…later…let the matter arise. Let all the cons arise: reasons, feelings, images…be aware of how it feels. Go away again. Do something else. Come back later. Let it arise and let a decision emerge. If still unclear, repeat the process. If still nothing, face the fact that a clear decision is not emerging and you'll have to respond as best you can with what clarity you've got.

7. Become still and quiet. Now express to yourself the decision or dedication you have reached with whatever words, images, expressions that are arising within you now. No matter the literary style, derivations, or form. Express what you mean and mean what you express. You may find it going beyond yourself, perhaps in the form of a prayer. Conventional or unconventional, let what you mean be expressed. Now imagine Mary, our Lady, listening to it. Imagine Jesus listening to it. Imagine the Father listening to your expressions. Be aware of how it all feels.

8. Now, when all is said and done, what are you actually going to do about it? When? Where and how? How do you feel about all that? Tell Mary; tell Jesus; tell the Father.

9. Let all strands of this fundamental option, this decision, this dedication, arise. Find the expression that seems appropriate now. What I really mean, what I really want to say with my own voice, and do with my own heart. Honestly and deeply as I see best, and express it now.

PRAYER EXERCISES

Number One: A Conversation with God

Quiet yourself and pray through this slowly. Let it take you into your own conversation with God.

Me: O God, there goes that thought again about becoming a sister (brother, priest). Why does it keep coming back?

God: Listen to it.

Me: After all that education, I finally got a job. Do you know how hard it is to get a job nowadays? And I am comfortable in my own place, driving my own car, enjoying my friends.

God: I can offer you more.

Me: Sure! A life without a family, in an institution, without the independence I have now. No way!

God: I only invite. I never coerce.

Me: That's what makes it so difficult. If you only gave me a crystal clear sign, something dramatic, then I wouldn't be so confused.

God: I am giving you signs. You enjoy your present ministry more than your job. There is a desire in you to give more of yourself and to have more meaning in your life.

VOCATIONS ANONYMOUS

Me: Well, I'm too afraid to get up in front of everybody and speak like the priests do. It takes too long to study to become a priest. It looks too lonely. And I'm afraid to commit myself to a religious community. What's their future? Do they know where they are going?

God: I will give you what you need. You will experience more love and affection from my people than you ever thought possible. You will see me work through your weakness and fears.

Me: All these thoughts scare me.

God: Give it careful thought. Keep me company. Sit with me when all the others have gone and you will see more clearly. Your desires will grow and your fears diminish.

Number Two: Naming God

There is a meditation recommended by Fr. Anthony De Mello, SJ, on "Names."[67] You may like to practice this meditation in order to become more intimately aware of who you are in relation to God through the names you call God and perhaps the names God calls you!

De Mello outlines this meditation in his book *Sadhana*. He invites you to invent names for Jesus as the psalmist invented names for God (Rock, King, or Warrior). He then invites you to imagine Jesus inventing names for you. Spend half an hour listening to the names God calls you (lover, friend, lost sheep, sinner, my delight…). Getting in touch with the power of names will help you better listen to the call and better respond because you will be in touch with who you really are.

[67] De Mello SJ, Anthony. *Sadhana*, P. 111 – 113.

PRAYER EXERCISES

Number Three: Journaling Fill-in the Blanks

In your notebook, complete the sentences below with your first gut response:

1. I am not sure about…

2. My greatest fear about being a sister/brother/priest is…

3. I doubt if…

4. I would enter a seminary or a novitiate tomorrow if only…

5. In ten years from now, I would like to be…

6. The gift or quality I would bring to a community (or to the priesthood) is…

Number Four: Journaling Reflections

Read through these questions and choose one or two that appeal to you. Reflect upon them and write down some of your responses in a journal.

1. Reflect upon your own particular life choice of a vocation (married, single, religious, or priestly). Was there a particular time when you felt "called" to this vocation? Can you identify any inner movements that helped you suspect that this lifestyle is for you?

2. Draw a line lengthwise across a sheet of paper. Write the year you were born on the left end of the line, and the present year on the far right. Recall significant moments when you sensed God calling you to further growth through people, prayer, events, job, or a life decision. Note them along with the years they occurred in the appropriate place on your timeline.

219

VOCATIONS ANONYMOUS

3. What challenges you most with regard to your call to be an active part of the Catholic Christian community?

4. How can you live out your call to discipleship, to follow Jesus in your particular lifestyle?

5. Psalm 18: 19 – 20 speaks of being saved because "God delighted in me." Spend some quiet time in meditation imagining that God delights in you. Listen. Let God love you and reveal how you are loved. Focus on a crucifix, an image, a mountain, or the ocean if it helps.

As you listen, are you aware of at least three ways in which God might delight in you? Are there any idiosyncrasies? What distinctive characteristics about you as a person gives God delight? For example, if you are a very inquisitive person, can you imagine God delighting in that aspect of your personality?

Number Five: Imagining Your Future

Sister Mary Neill, OP, during an Integration Seminar at the University of San Francisco, suggested this meditation. In this meditation, you imagine that God comes to you before you are born. God tells you that there is something that needs to be addressed in the present time, this particular century. God shows you the particular culture, geographical location, and time of history into which you will be born. God also shows you the unique personality, body, and temperament that will be yours. Perhaps there is a disability, or a painful childhood, or a dysfunctional family setting. All of this will gift you with a particular wound. The gospel needs to be preached in your time, and through this particular wound, you will be able to preach the Gospel.

PRAYER EXERCISES

Can you say to God, "Behold, I come to do your will"? Can you accept the particular circumstances of your life? It is as if God has prepared you to witness to the gospel through who you are and your life history. "I have prepared you as a polished arrow and hid you in my quiver" (Psalm 49: 2). This wound enables me to share the wisdom that the world may need to hear.

This exercise can enable us to see our weakness as a medium for God's strength and power. God calls us as we are. We can take that to mean that God calls us *in spite of* our weaknesses. I prefer to think that God calls us *because of* those very weaknesses. Perhaps Peter's impulsiveness gave him the impetus to make the courageous choices later on in his life. I firmly believe that whatever our personal deficits, weakness, family history or baggage, *all* will be used in ministry somehow, someday. Effective ministers are often people who have gone through struggles with an addiction or did recovery work through ACOA and 12-step programs. This experience suits them well for ministry to an addictive society. It can also free them from the "victim mentality" which could inhibit a free response to God's call. Dealing with personal issues in counseling is very important. Surrender and moving forward as one is healed is critical to personal growth. Paul, for example, experienced personal weakness as a medium for God's power and strength. God promised him (and promises us) "My grace is enough for you, for in weakness power reached perfection." Paul grew to understand that "when I am powerless, it is then that I am strong." (2 Corinthians 12: 9 – 10)

Number Six: The Elements of Call

Read Luke 1: 26 – 38 (Mary's Call) and Acts 9: 10 – 19 (Ananias' Call).

221

VOCATIONS ANONYMOUS

Each story reveals a pattern:

1. God invites

2. The person hesitates

3. God makes a promise

4. The person consents

Can you find these elements in Mary's Call in Luke's Gospel as well as Ananias' Call in Acts? Do you experience a similar pattern in your own life? If so, where are you in that process? Do you find yourself hesitating? Listening? Consenting?

Number Seven: Freedom and Un-freedom

Knowing yourself well helps in the movement toward inner freedom. Do you know the areas of *un-freedom* in your life? Reflect on areas of un-freedom and be able to name them for yourself. It may help to write them down. To help you begin, here are some common areas of un-freedom.

Possessions? (If there were a fire, what would I save?)

Desire for status?

Attachment to opinions?

Prejudices?

Need to control?

Relationships?

Routine? My *modus operandi*?

Who do I try to impress?

One clue to your un-freedoms would be those things that eat up your energy and dissipate your focus. If you have a prayer partner or spiritual director, you may want to share these areas of un-freedom so that you can be challenged during the discernment process if you slip into one or the other. The sacrament of Reconciliation can be a way to keep a check on areas of life that need healing in the growth towards freedom.

Number Eight: Holy Desires

Pray with John 1: 35 – 39, the passage in which some disciples are curious about Jesus and follow him. Jesus turns around and confronts them with the question, "What are you looking for?" Imagine that you are following Jesus at a "safe distance." Visualize Jesus turning around, looking you in the eye, and asking:

"What is it that you really desire?"

"What is it that you are looking for in life?"

"What do you really want?"

Off the top of your head, you may have ready answers, but go deeper. Spend time with the question. Spend some quality time listening and allowing your deepest desires to emerge. What gets stirred up within you? You may pray with this passage over a few weeks and return to it several times. Give yourself the space to be present to the Word of God as presented in Jesus' question.

Part of the purpose of this meditation is to get in touch with your personal fears and doubts about a new direction or call in your life. Where is the resistance? Make sure that you bring each and every reaction and feeling before God in prayer. Resistance is always an invitation to go deeper and through to the other side. Anything which strongly attracts or repels us is indicative of an area in which we need further growth and exploration.

An example of resistance from my own life might highlight this dynamic for you. In 1979, I was teaching high school in Ireland. The agreement was for one year. My superior in California wrote asking me to discern a future ministry when I returned the following year to California. I began praying and was suddenly struck by a text of scripture that went straight to the heart. "Leave your country, your kinsfolk and your father's house for the land which I will show you" (Genesis 12:1). I was so resistant to any suggestion that I might not return home that I stopped praying for a few weeks. I did go to chapel with the sisters for Mass and prayer several times a day, but I deliberately didn't listen or honestly pray. A few weeks later, I figured I had to start praying again so that I would have some response for my superior.

For the next few months, I kept hearing an invitation to move on. It invited me to take a risk, to let go. The only other geographical place that came to mind was Africa. My resistance grew. I was a former piano music major and lacked the outdoor skills of a Girl Scout! I wouldn't do well in a rural environment, or so I told God. I came from the beaches of Southern California. What could God do with me in Africa?

After a few months, I noticed my resistance waned. As I prayed honestly with all of my fears and doubts, my heart was turned around 180 degrees. My spiritual director thought that this idea of moving on could be my imagination so he warned me not to volunteer for the "missions." I didn't, but when God moved me into the right frame of mind and heart, I was asked to go to Zambia. This is just an example of how working with resistance can be life changing. I had the best five years of my life in Zambia.

Reflect on the following questions after having prayed the passage from John. They may help point you to a particular ministry or vocation.

- What is most life-giving for me right now?

- Where is my deepest desire?

- What are my gifts, personal qualities? Where am I best suited to serve?

- What do I hear God saying?

- If I were on my deathbed, which choice would I wish I'd have made?[68]

- What motives are influencing me to choose one vocation over another?

Some very important signs to pay attention to in your life that may indicate a change of direction or another vocation to serve would be:

- A gentle nudge or tug pointing to a particular vocation or ministry

- A recurring thought that you have dismissed time and time again

- Comments and advice from those who know you regarding your abilities, gifts and future.

Notice how you resist God's invitation by refusing to look at something - as I did in the previous example. Also pay attention to those times in your life where you may avoid prayer and seek out other comforts: escape into work,

---

[68] St. Ignatius of Loyola. The second week of the Spiritual Exercises.

VOCATIONS ANONYMOUS

movies, books, relationships, or sleep, for example, can be forms of resistance.

St. Ignatius of Loyola practiced "holy daydreaming" in which he imagined himself doing great things for God. He would fantasize about undertaking challenging and difficult feats for God. Anthony De Mello recommends a meditation called "Holy Desires" in his book, *Sadhana*.[69] In it you pray about the holy desire you have for others as well as the great desires you have for yourself. De Mello encourages you to imagine the great deeds of some of the saints and make those deeds your own through desire.

Number Nine: The Ebb and Flow of the Spirits

Reflect on the following questions about discerning spirits. With a prayer partner or spiritual director, share the movements and counter–movements that you are aware of in your life – the ebb and flow of the spirits.

Anxiety	Peace
Possessiveness	Inclusiveness
Jealousy	Flexibility
Competition	Concern for others, charity
Desire to control	Service
Boredom	Fidelity
Restlessness, hatred, fear, and self-pity	Joy, wonder, gratitude
Sterility	Life
Prejudice	Openness
Resistance to creative options	Tension (anger over injustice)

---

[69] De Mello SJ, Anthony. *Sadhana: A Way to God,* pp. 126 – 128.

PRAYER EXERCISES

- Does my desire to serve or relate come from the Holy Spirit, or am I moved by egocentric interests?

- Am I docile, or do I have a need to control?

- What cultural/societal influences steer me away from God?

- What patterns lead me toward life and create a fertile environment for God's grace?

- Given that my orientation is toward God and my life is in harmony with that direction, where do I experience peace versus turmoil?

Some motivating factors that can influence decisions and choices are:

- Money, convenience, pleasure, power, appearance, what others may think of me

OR

- Gospel values, virtues, evangelization, service to the community, gifts and fruits of the Spirit in my life.

When you are discerning a vocation to priesthood or religious life, there are specific tugs and pulls that you want to be aware of:

- Would you feel "special" if you were to be a priest, sister, or brother? Examine the roots of this motivation. Is there a hidden desire for status, recognition, privilege?

- An energizing, impelling desire to preach the Gospel in a relevant way so that people can really hear the message of Jesus in our time?

- A desire for security? Perhaps you look forward to being

227

a priest or religious because you know you will always have a job and a place to live. A more subtle form of this would be that you don't trust yourself to really attend to your spiritual life and feel that if you were in a convent or seminary, that prayer would be part of the routine of daily life.

- You are lonely. Perhaps you feel that developing a relationship is difficult. People expect to be sexually involved and you don't believe in sex outside of marriage. You can't find anyone with your values and love for God. Entering a seminary or religious community would enable you to have "instant" friends. Beware! Developing relationships is an adult skill that must be in place before you enter!

- The plight of the poor and homeless has motivated you to take action. You can no longer be true to yourself and not get involved. You explore communities with a ministry or charism to serve the poor with dignity.

A spiritual director can be invaluable in helping you to recognize which spirit may be at work in your motivations and desires. Spiritual direction will also help you grow in awareness of your own particular vulnerabilities. Some people are prone to poor self-esteem, others to pride. Depending on your own personal tendency you can be drawn into desolation. Know your weak areas well and you'll be one step ahead of the devil!

Number Ten: Remembering the Experience of God

Some suggestions for meditation:

Psalms 25, 103, 107 & 139   *Deuteronomy 1: 29 - 33*
Proverbs 3: 3   *Sirach 2: 1 - 18*
John 4   *Ephesians 3*

Recall a significant experience of God. Remember the time and the place. What was your life situation at the time? Were you a student, working, married, single? Relive the details of how you encountered God or how God found you. Spend time savoring the details of this experience. After a period of reflection, ask yourself:

• What did I experience?

• Who was God for me in this experience?

• How has that memory or experience shaped my decisions since?

• How is that incident a hallmark in my life?

• How do I make decisions out of this experience of God?

In time of desolation, return to the memory of a consoling experience such as the one you chose for this exercise.

VOCATIONS ANONYMOUS

Number Eleven: Celibacy Test

YES	NO	
		I have close friends. Some of my friends are my peers (around my own age, similar education and social circle).
		I have a life!
		I can enjoy time alone.
		I can set limits.
		I have a personal relationship with God and my prayer time is one of intimacy with this God.
		I can say "No."
		I am willing to love those no one else will love.
		I don't need to satisfy my own needs immediately. I can delay gratification.
		My social circle is a mix of men and women.
		My prayer life supports my struggle to be chaste.
		I know how to be intimate without being active sexually.
		I have made and kept commitments in my life.
		I can be honest, down to earth, realistic, joyful, and warm (though not all of the time! We're not perfect!)
		Most of the time I am comfortable with my own body and emotions.

PRAYER EXERCISES

Number Twelve: Intimacy with Self

How well do you really know yourself? Answer "yes" or "no" to the following statements.

YES	NO	
		I am able to identify my feelings by name.
		I enjoy having time alone to reflect, relax, pray.
		I know what I am afraid of.
		I am aware of my reactions to people, places and things that upset me.
		I know my deepest joys.
		I know who I am.
		I am familiar and comfortable with my cultural back ground and roots.
		My family heritage and traits are in my awareness.
		I remember my childhood.
		I remember a time when God touched me in a very personal way.
		I can sense God reaching out to me even though subtly and quietly.
		I know how I will respond under pressure and stress.
		I know what relaxes me.
		I can observe myself growing through my relationships with God and with other people.
		I know what causes me to be sensitive and defensive.
		I can laugh at myself, my mistakes, my foolishness.

231

VOCATIONS ANONYMOUS

YES	NO	
		I experience growing in freedom in knowing how much I am loved and how valuable I am.
		My importance rests on who I am and not on what I do.
		My life's direction is consistent with my values.
		I have some goals in mind and some ways of achieving them.
		I know where I am most vulnerable in a relationship.
		I notice which compliments touch me most deeply.
		I feel safe and content.
		I am comfortable expressing my feelings.
		I am comfortable with my body and I know how it responds.

Number Thirteen: Discernment Examen[70]

This is a simple prayer exercise which can help you become more aware. I call it a discernment examen. It takes five to ten minutes, preferably prayed in the evening, and it goes like this:

1. Relax in the presence of God; be aware of God's loving presence in and all around you.

2. Thank God for everything that has been loved into your life since yesterday's examen.

---

[70] Used with permission from Fr. Armand Nigro, SJ.

PRAYER EXERCISES

3.   Beg to be given "the mind and heart of Christ" to see reality as Jesus sees it.

4.   Reflect prayerfully over your day; go through the day with the Lord, checking the "we" (what you and Jesus experience together) against the "I" (you alone), Jesus lives in us so we can say, as St. Paul does, "I live not myself alone but Christ lives in me" (Gal. 2: 19). This means that in reality, you live as a "we" (you and God), not just an "I."

As you reflect over the day, then, see everything about which you can say "we" (even if you were not conscious of God's presence at the time). For example, "We ate breakfast, we drove to work, we cleaned the house, we spent time with people, we rested, etc."

As we prayerfully reflect over our day in this way, God sensitizes us to the ways in which God touches us and is present to us all during the day. In other words, God enables us to "discern" or diagnose God's touch from all the other movements and urges in our lives.

The focus of our attention is on God and God's presence – not just on us. That's why I call it a "discernment examen." This helps us become more aware of God's presence throughout the day. It helps us to integrate our faith into our daily lives, to be more confident and peaceful about doing God's will.

5.   Renew in love our sorrow for any way we fell short or were not our best selves. Make up your own personal prayer for any weakness or sinfulness you experienced that day.

6.   Accept an invitation from God to spend some time in

prayer tomorrow. Make it a date with a definite place and length of time. And accept any invitation God gives to repair any damage or behave better the next time we face the kind of situation which occasioned our fall.

7.   End by praying the Lord's Prayer slowly.

If you stick to this prayer period or discernment examen for five minutes each day, you will experience growth in the sensitivity to God's presence and be more responsive to God's invitations.

PRAYER EXERCISES

Number Fourteen: Prayer of Abandonment

BY CHARLES DE FOUCAULD

Father
I abandon myself into your hands;
Do with me what you will.
Whatever you may do, I thank you;
I am ready for all, I accept all.
Let only your will be done in me,
And in all your creatures.
I wish no more than this, O Lord.
Into your hands I commend my soul;
I offer it to you
With all the love of my heart,
For I love you, Lord,
And so need to give myself,
To surrender myself into you hands
Without reserve,
And with boundless confidence,
For you are my Father.

Number Fifteen: Prayer of St. Ignatius

Dearest Jesus, teach me to be generous, teach me to love and serve you as you deserve, to give and not to count the cost, to fight and not to heed the wounds, to toil and not to seek for rest; to labor and to look for no reward save that of knowing that I do your holy will.

235

VOCATIONS ANONYMOUS

ONLINE RESOURCES

YouTube Videos

Pray! Listen! Act! Repeat! Youtube video on discernment at
http://www.youtube.com/watch?v=jppsxDQp0jU

For the Sake of the Call by Steven Curtis Chapman
http://www.youtube.com/watch?v=1sb4RrF9VxI

Jesus Calls Women
http://www.youtube.com/watch?v=vFfDXN1Ieyo

A Different Path (about Catholic nuns)
https://www.youtube.com/watch?v=dqq1nWjLd-o

Here I Am
https://www.youtube.com/watch?v=7vNsAmf53mM

Young Beautiful Actress left Hollywood to be a Cloistered Nun
https://www.youtube.com/watch?v=BKGmDifYq60

John Paul 2 on Vocations and Holiness
http://www.youtube.com/watch?feature=player_detailpage&v=KnI3Z_aCIDM

Three keys to vocation discernment by Vision Vocation Guide
http://www.youtube.com/watch?feature=player_detailpage&v=O03LVg2M-Uo

A Woman's Vocation Story (Juliet Mousseau RSCJ)
http://www.youtube.com/watch?feature=player_detailpage&v=uxkCorOWE9A

Four steps to discerning God's will
http://www.youtube.com/watch?feature=player_detailpage&v=0CDQZNDFylQ

Go to YouTube and search vocation stories like this one:
"A Special Vision" Fr. Larry Gillick SJ
https://www.youtube.com/watch?v=frtpyWhuWzg

Podcasts:

A Nun's Life
www.anunslife.org

Pray as You Go
http://www.pray-as-you-go.org

Sacred Music By DJ Phyre
http://vocationnetwork.org/articles/show/346

Blogs:

You can sign up to receive daily inspirations!

- *http://www.godinallthings.com*

- **Finding God Everyday:**
  Everything Is Holy Now is written by Charis'
  National Partners Coordinator, Becky El-
  dredge, about finding God every day.
  http://everythingisholynow.blogspot.com

- **Whosoever Desires** engages with the greater community
  from the perspective of several young Jesuits at:
  http://whosoeverdesires.wordpress.com

- **Jesuit Collaborative Blog** offers reflections and gives us
  resources for entering into Ignatian prayer on a regular
  basis.
  http://jesuit-collaborative.org/tjc-journal

ONLINE RESOURCES

- **Stay Great** was started by Fr. Mark Link, SJ, and reinforces that God made all of us great. *Staygreat.com*

- **Googling God** Author, editor and dog-lover Mike Hayes blogs his experience in the young adult Catholic world. *googlingGod.com*

Websites to learn how to pray with Scripture:

Sacred Space
http://www.sacredspace.ie

Daily Reflections on the Scripture:
http://onlineministries.creighton.edu/
CollaborativeMinistry/online.html

Busted Halo
http://bustedhalo.com

Pray the Liturgy of the Hours at
http://www.universalis.com

3 minute Retreats:
http://www.loyolapress.com

Spiritual Exercises at
http://jesuits.org/spirituality?PAGE=DTN-20130520125429

Other Websites:

Charis Ministries:
http://charisministries.org for those in their
20's and 30's nurturing their faith

Great Story of a Maryknoll Priest
http://www.maryknollsociety.org

Vocationcast is an English site with modern music, link to iTunes etc – Abbot Jamison
http://vocationcast.org/about

239

VOCATIONS ANONYMOUS

RESOURCE BIBLIOGRAPHY

Resources to support your discernment process, organized according to topic

Vocation Discernment

Au, Wilkie and Noreen Cannon Au. *The Discerning Heart: Exploring the Christian Path*, Mahweh, New Jersey, Paulist Press, 2006.

Aridas, *Chris. Discernment: Seeking God in Every Situation.* Locust Valley, NY: Living Flame. 1981.

Barry, SJ, William A. *Paying Attention to God: Discernment in Prayer.* Notre Dame: Ave Maria Press. 1990.

Bryant, Kathleen. *All For Love* (Readings and Journal for Young Adults Discerning Their Life Call).

Bryant, Kathleen. *On The Way to Priesthood,* an interactive journal for men discerning their vocation.

Bryant, Kathleen. *Discern Mission and Ministry*; A tool for teaching discernment to lay ministers and leadership at the parish.

Cameli, Lous, Robert Miller, and Gerard P. Weber. *A Sense of Direction: The Basic Elements of the Spiritual Journey.* Valencia, CA: Tabor Publications. 1987.

Conroy, Maureen. *The Discerning Heart: Discovering a Personal God*, Chicago, Loyola Press, 1993.

Green, SJ, Thomas. *Weeds Among the Wheat.* Notre Dame: Ave Maria Press. 1984.

Himes, Michael *Doing the Truth in Love*, Mahwah, New Jersey, Paulist Press, 1995.

Knobbe, Beth. *Finding My Voice: A Young Woman's Perspective (Called to Holiness)*, St. Anthony Messenger, 2009.

Liebert, Elizabeth, SNJM. *The Way of Discernment: Spiritual Practices for Decision Making*, Louisville, KY, Westminster John Knox Press, 2008.

Lonsdale, David *Listening to the Music of the Spirit: The Art of Discernment,* Notre Dame, IN, Ave Maria Press, 1993.

Martin, James, SJ. *Becoming Who You Are: Insights on the True Self from Thomas Merton and Other Saints,* Mahweh, New Jersey, Paulist Press, 2006.

Martin, James, SJ. *In Good Company The Fast Track from the Corporate World to Poverty, Chastity, and Obedience* Chicago, Sheed and Ward, Rowman & Littlefield 10th Anniversary Edition 2010.

Mossa, Mark, SJ. *Already There Letting God Find You*, St. Anthony Messenger Press, 2010.

Nemeck, Francis. K. and Coombs, Marie T. *Called by God: A Theology of Vocation and Lifelong Commitment.* Collegeville: Liturgical Press. 1992.

Nouwen, Henri. *Wounded Healer.* NY: Image Books. 1990.

Oliva, Max, SJ. *Free to Love, Free to Pray* Notre Dame, IN: Ave Maria Press, 1994.

Pennington, OCSO, Basil. *Called: New Thinking on Christian Vocation.* Minneapolis: Seabury Press. 1983.

RESOURCE BIBLIOGRAPHY

Silf, Margaret and Gerald W. Hughes. *The Inner Compass: An Invitation to Ignatian Spirituality*, Chicago, Loyola Press, 1999.

Silf, Margaret. *Wise Choices: A Spiritual Guide to Making Life's Decisions,* Bluebridge, 2007.

Sparough, J. Michael. *What's Your Decision?* How to Make Choices with Confidence and Clarity: An Ignatian Approach to Decision Making, Chicago, Loyola Press, 2010.

Whitehead, James and Evelyn. *Seasons of Strength: New Visions of Adult Christian Maturing.* Winona, MN: St. Mary's Press. 1995.

Wolff, Pierre. *Discernment: The Art of Choosing Well.* Liguori, MO: Triumph Books. 1993.

Adult Children of Alcoholics/Codependency Issues

Beattie, Melody. *Codependent No More: How to Stop Controlling Others and Start Caring for Yourself.* San Francisco: Harper. 1992.

Black, Claudia. *It Will Never Happen to Me.* NY: Ballantine Books. 1987.

Bradshaw, John. *Healing the Shame that Binds You.* Deerfield Beach, FL: Health Communications, Inc. 1988.

Woititz, Janet Geringer. *Adult Children of Alcoholics.* Deerfield Beach, FL: Health Communications, Inc. 1990.

Catholic Faith

Bokenkotter, Thomas. *Dynamic Catholicism,* Image Publishers, 1986.

Clark, Bishop Edward. *Five Great Catholic Ideas,* NY, Crossroad Publishing Company, 1998.

Huebsch, Bill. *The Constitutions (Vatican II in Plain English),* Notre Dame, IN, Ave Maria Press, 2008.

Huebsch, Bill. Quick Reference Guide, The Documents of Vatican II (Google this for the guide; available in Spanish and English).

Pennock, Michael Francis. *This is Our Faith.* Notre Dame: Ave Maria Press. 1989.

Pollard, John. *Exploring Your Catholic Faith: Basic Teaching and Practices,* Allen, RX, RCL Benzinger, 1996.

Rausch, Thomas, SJ. *The College Student's Introduction to Theology,* Liturgical Press, 1993.

Rausch, Thomas, SJ. *Educating for Faith and Justice,* The Liturgical Press, 2010.

Schreck, Alan. *Basics of the Faith: A Catholic Catechism.* Ann Arbor, MI: Servant Books, 1987.

Wilhelm, Anthony. *Christ Among Us: A Modern Presentation of the Catholic Faith for Adults.* 5th rev. ed. San Francisco: Harper Collins. 1990.

The Catechism of the Catholic Church. Washington, DC: National Catholic Conference of Catholic Bishops. 1994.

Celibacy

Clarke, Keith. *Being Sexual and Celibate: An Experience of Celibacy.* Notre Dame: Ave Maria Press. 1982.

Huddleston, IHM, Mary Anne. *Celibate Loving: Encounter in Three Dimension.* NY: Paulist Press. 1984.

Keane, Philip. *Sexual Morality: A Catholic Perspective.* NY: Paulist Press. 1977.

Martini, Carlo Maria. *On the Body: A Contemporary Theology of the Human Person*, NY: Crossroad, 2001.

Nelson, James B. *The Intimate Connection: Male Sexuality, Masculine Spirituality.* 1st ed. Philadelphia: Westminster Press. 1988.

Nouwen, Henri. *Lifesigns: Intimacy, Fecundity, and Ecstasy in Christian Perspective.* NY: Doubleday. 1989.

Whitehead, Evelyn Easton and James. *A Sense of Sexuality: Christian Love and Intimacy.* NY: Crossroad. 1994.

Christology

O'Collins, SJ, Gerald. *Interpreting Jesus.* Introducing Catholic Theology, Vol. 2. Ramsey, NJ: Paulist Press. 1983.

Delio, Ilia. *The Emergent Christ,* NY, Orbis, 2011.

Church Documents

Pope John Paul II, *Vita Consecrata*

Huebsch, Bill. Quick Reference Guide, The Documents of Vatican II (Google this for the guide; available in Spanish and English).

Confoy, Maryanne, RSC. *Religious Life and Priesthood: Perfectae Caritatis, Optatam Totius, Presbyterorum Ordinis* (Rediscovering Vatican II), Mahwah, NJ, Paulist Press, 2008.

Building Economic Justice: The Bishops' Pastoral Letter and Tools for Action. Washington, DC: National Catholic Conference of Catholic Bishops, 1987.

Building Peace: A Pastoral Reflection on the Response to the "Challenge of Peace." Washington, DC: National Catholic Conference of Catholic Bishops. 1988.

Path From Puebla: Significant Documents of the Latin American Bishops since 1979. Edward L. Clearly, Ed. Washington, DC: Secretariat, Bishops Committee for the Church in Latin America. National Catholic Conference of Catholic Bishops. 1989.

Encuentro Nacional Hispano de Pastoral 1985. *Prophetic Voices: The Document on the Process of the III Encuentro Nacional de Pastoral Hispano.* Washington, DC: 1986.

Documents of Aparecida, Conference of Catholic Bishops of Latin America, 2007.

Church History

Bokenkotter, Thomas. *A Concise History of the Catholic Church.* Garden City, NY: Doubleday. 1977.

Comby, Jean, and Diarmaid MacCullock. *How to Read Church History.* 2 vols. London: SCM Press. 1985.

Holmes, Derek *A Short History of the Catholic Church*, Burns & Oates 2002.

Ecclesiology

Boff, Leonardo. *Ecclesiogenesis: The Base Communities Reinvent the Church.* Robert Barr, trans. Maryknoll, NY: Orbis Books. 1986.

Crosby, Michael. *Spirituality of the Beatitudes: Matthew's Challenge for First World Christians.* Maryknoll, NY: Orbis Books. 1981.

Lawlor, Michael and Thomas Shanahan. *Church: A Spiritual Communion,* Collegeville, MN , *Liturgical Press, 1995.*

Tavard, George. *The Church, Community of Salvation,* Collegeville, MN , *Liturgical Press, 1992.*

Whitehead, James and Evelyn Easton. *Emerging Laity: Returning Leadership to the Community of Faith.* NY: Doubleday. 1988.

Healing Sexual Abuse

Bass, Ellen and Laura Davis. *The Courage to Heal: A Guide for Women Survivors of Child Sexual Abuse.* 3rd Ed. NY: Harper Perennial. 1994.

Black-Grubman, Stephen. *Broken Boys, Mending Men: Recovery from Childhood Sexual Abuse.* NY: Ivy Books. 1992.

Engel, Beverly. *Outgrowing the Pain* (Help for women who were abused as children), NC, Ivy Books, 1990.

Gil, Eliana. *Outgrowing the Pain: Help for Women Who Were Abused as Children.* Lunch Press, PO Box 3141, Walnut Creek, CA 94598.

Hunt, Meg. *Abused Boys: Neglected Victims of Sexual Abuse.* NY: *Fawcett* Columbine. 1991.

Jarema, William J. *There's a Hole in My Chest, Healing & Hope for Adult Children Everywhere,* NY, Crossroad, 1996.

Klausner, Mary Ann & Bobbie Hasselbring. *Aching for Love: The Sexual Drama of the Adult Child.* San Francisco: Harper Row. 1990.

Lew, Mike. *Victims No Longer: Men Recovering from Incest and Other Sexual Child Abuse.* NY: Perennial Library. 1990.

Linn, Dennis and Linn, Matthew. *Healing Life's Hurts: Healing of Memories Through Five Steps of Forgiveness.* NY: Paulist Press. 1978.

Sanford, John A. *Healing and Wholeness.* NY: Paulist Press. 1977.

Life Changes

Au, Wilkie. *The Enduring Heart: Spirituality for the Long Haul*, Mahwah, NJ, Paulist Press, 2000.

Brennan, Anne and Janice Brewi. *Midlife Directions: Praying and Playing Sources of New Dynamism.* NY: Paulist Press. 1986.

Dyckman, SNJM, Katherine and L. Patrick Carroll. *Chaos or Creation: Spirituality in Midlife.* NY: Paulist Press. 1986.

Sheehy, Gail. *Passages: Predictable Crisis of Adult Life.* NY: Bantam Books, 1981.

Silf, Margaret. *The Other Side of Chaos: Breaking Through When Life Is Breaking Down*, Loyola Press, 2011.

Whitehead, James and Evelyn. *Christian Life Patterns: The Psychological Challenges and Religious Invitations of Adult Life.* NY: Crossroads. 1992.

Mary

Brown, Raymond, et. al. *Mary in the New Testament.* Philadelphia: Fortress Press. 1978.

Pennington, OCSO, Basil. *Mary Today: The Challenging Woman.* 1st Image ed. NY: Doubleday. 1989.

Tambasco, Anthony J. *What Are They Saying About Mary?* NY: Paulist Press. 1984.

Prayer

The Cloud of Unknowing: A New Translation of a Classic Guide to Spiritual Experience. Ira Progoff, trans. NY: Delta. 1989.

Barry, SJ, William A. *God and You.* NY: Paulist Press. 1987.

Barry, William A. *Praying the Truth: Deepening Your Friendship with God through Honest Prayer.*

Brook, John *School of Prayer* (An Introduction to the Divine Office).

Carroll, Patrick and Katherine Dychman, SNJM. *Inviting the Mystic, Supporting the Prophet.*

Hall, Thelma. *Too Deep for Words: Rediscovering Lectio Divina.* NY: Paulist Press. 1988.

Hart, Thomas N. *The Art of Christian Listening.* NY: Paulist Press. 1980.

Hughes, Gerard W. *God of Surprises.* Cambridge, MA: Cowley Publications. 1993. Previously published by Paulist Press, 1972.

Martin, James, SJ. *Together on Retreat (Meeting Jesus in Prayer* [Kindle Edition With Audio/Video], 2013.

Merton, Thomas. *Seeds of Contemplation.* NY: New Directions. 1986.

Contemplative Prayer. Introduction of Thich Nhat Han. NY: Image Books. 1996.

Pennington, OCSO, Basil. *Call to the Center: The Gospel's Invitation to Deeper Prayer.* Hyde Park, NY: New City Press. 1995.

_____. *The Way Back Home: An Introduction to Centering Prayer.* NY: Paulist Press. 1989.

_____. *Centered Living: The Way of Centering Prayer.* NY: Doubleday. 1988.

Steindl-Rast, OSB, David. *Grateful, The Heart of Prayer: An Approach to Life in Fullness.* NY: Paulist Press. 1984.

Priesthood

Beck, Edward. *God Underneath: Spiritual Memoirs of a Catholic Priest*, CO, Image Books, 2002.

Bryant, Kathleen. *On The Way to Priesthood,* a journal for men discerning priesthood.

Cozzens, Donald B. *The Spirituality of the Diocesan Priest*, Collegeville, MN: Liturgical Press, 1997.

Dolan, Timothy. *Priesthood for the 3rd Millennium*, IN, Our Sunday Visitor, 2000.

Dulles, Avery. *The Priestly Office: A Theological Reflection*, NJ, Paulist Press, 1997.

Duquin, Christopher. *Could You Ever Become a Catholic Priest?* NY, Alba House, 1998.

Friedle, Francis P. and Rex Reynolds. *Extraordinary Lives*, 34 Priests Tell Their Stories, Notre Dame: Ave Maria Press, 1998.

RESOURCE BIBLIOGRAPHY

Hennessey, Paul. *A Concert of Charisms,* Ordained Ministry in the Religious Life, NJ, Paulist Press, 1997.

Kunkel, Thomas. *Enormous Prayers, NY,* Basic Books, 1999.

O'Malley, William. *The Fifth Week*, Chicago, Loyola Press, 1998.

Philibert, Paul J. *The Priesthood of the Faithful: Key to a Living Church*, Collegeville, MN, Liturgical Press, 2005.

Rausch, Thomas. *Priesthood Today: An Appraisal.* NY: Paulist Press. 1992.

Rossetti, Stephen. *The Joy of Priesthood*, Ave Maria Press, Indiana, 2005.

Rossetti, Stephen. *Why Priests are Happy,* Ave Maria Press, Indiana, 2011.

Osborne, Kenan. *Priesthood: A History of Ordained Ministry in the Roman Catholic Church.* NY: Paulist Press. 1989.

Religious Life

Carroll, Patrick, SJ. *To Love, To Share, To Serve: Challenges to a Religious,* Collegeville, MN The Liturgical Press, 1979.

Chittister, Joan. *The Fire in These Ashes:* A Spirituality of Contemporary Religious Life, Kansas City, MO , Sheed and Ward, 1995.

Fiand, Barbara. *Living the Vision: Religious Vows in an Age of Change.* NY: Crossroads. 1990.

Fiand, Barbara. *Wrestling With God*, NY, the Crossroad Publishing Company, 1996.

Francis, Mother Mary. *A Right to be Merry (About the Life of a Poor Clare Nun*) (Ignatius Press) *http://www.ignatius.com/promotions/mmfrancis/*

Hennessey, Paul. *A Concert of Charisms,* Ordained Ministry in the Religious Life, NJ, Paulist Press, 1997.

Leng, Felicity. *Consecrated Spirits*, A thousand years of spiritual writings by women religious, London, Canterbury Press, 2011.

Martin, James. *In Good Company: The Fast Track from the Corporate World to Poverty, Chastity, and Obedience, Kansas City, MO; Sheed and Ward, 2010.*

Schneiders, Sandra. *New Wineskins: Re-imagining Religious Life Today.* NY: Paulist Press. 1986.

> *Buying the Field: Catholic Religious Life in Mission to the World,* 2013.

> *Finding the Treasure: Locating Catholic Religious Life in a New Ecclesial and Cultural Text*, 2000.

> *Selling All: Commitment, Consecrated Celibacy, and Community in Catholic Religious Life*, 2001.

Turpin, Joanne. *Women in Church History: 20 Stories for 20 Centuries.* Cincinnati: St. Anthony Messenger Press. 1990.

Woodward, Evelyn. *Poets, Prophets and Pragmatists: A New Challenge to Religious Life.* Notre Dame: Ave Maria Press. 1987.

Sacramental Theology

Guzie, Tad. *The Book of Sacramental Basics.* NY: Paulist Press. 1981.

Hellwig, Monika K. *The Eucharist and the Hunger of the World.* 2nd ed., rev. and expanded. Kansas City: Sheed & Ward. 1992.

Huebsch, Bill. *Re-thinking the Sacraments: Holy Moments in Daily Living.* Mystics, CT: Twenty-Third Publications. 1989.

Mick, Lawrence. *Understanding the Sacraments Today.* Collegeville, MN: Liturgical Press. 1987.

Osborne, OFM, Kenan B. *The Christian Sacraments of Initiation: Baptism, Confirmation, Eucharist.* NY: Paulist Press. 1987.

Scripture

The Catholic Study Bible (Daily readings so you cover the entire Bible) Oxford University Press.

Boadt, CSP, Lawrence. *Reading the Old Testament: An Introduction.* NY: Paulist Press. 1984.

Brown, Robert McAfee. *Unexpected News: Reading the Bible with Third World Eyes.* Philadelphia: Westminster Press. 1984.

Hann, Robert R. *The Bible: An Owner's Manual. What You Need to Know Before You Buy and Read Your Bible.* NY: Paulist Press. 1983.

Keegan, Terence J. *Interpreting the Bible: A Popular Introduction to Biblical Hermeneutics.* NY: Paulist Press. 1985.

Marinelli, Anthony J. *Understanding the Gospels: A Guide for Beginners.* NY: Paulist Press. 1988.

Perkins, Pheme. *Hearing the Parables of Jesus: Reading the New Testament.* NY: Paulist Press. 1981.

Social Issues

Dear, SJ, John. *Disarming the Heart: Toward a Vow of Non-violence.* Scottdale, PA: Herald Press. 1993.

Gallagher, Vincent A. *"The True Cost of Low Prices - The Violence of Globalization"*, NY, Orbis, 2006.

Gutierrez, Gustavo. *On Job: God Talk and the Suffering of the Innocent.* Maryknoll, NY: Orbis Books. 1987.

Gutierrez, Gustavo. *We Drink from Our Own Wells: The Spiritual Journey of a People.* Maryknoll, NY: Orbis Books. 1984.

Spirituality

Au, Wilkie. *By way of the heart: Toward a holistic Christian spirituality*, NJ, Paulist Press, 1991.

Au, Wilkie and Noreen Cannon. *Urgings of the Heart: A Spirituality of Integration*, NJ, Paulist, Press, 1996.

Baron, Robert. *The Strangest Way,* NY, Orbis, 2002.

Barry, SJ, William A. *God's Passionate Desire and Our Response.* Notre Dame: Ave Maria Press. 1993.

Broccolo, Gerard, and Susan B. Thompson. *Vital Spiritualities.* Notre Dame: Ave Maria Press. 1990.

Brother Lawrence. *The Practice of the Presence of God, PA, Whitaker House, 1982.*

Cannato, Judy. *Field of Compassion: How the New Cosmology Is Transforming Spiritual Life*, Notre Dame: Sorin Books, 2010.

Cannato, Judy. *Radical Amazement: Contemplative Lessons from Black Holes, Supernovas, and Other Wonders of the Universe,* Notre Dame: Sorin Books, 2006.

Caprio, Betsy and Thomas M. Hedberg. *At a Dream Workshop.* NY: Paulist Press. 1987.

Teilhard de Chardin. Pierre. *The Divine Milieu.* NY: Harper 1968.

Clemmons, William. *Discovering the Depths.* Nashville: Broadman Press. 1987.

Cooper, Terry D. *Accepting the Troll Underneath the Bridge, Overcoming Self Doubts*, OR, Wipf & Stock Pub, 2010.

De Caussade, Jean-Pierre. *Abandonment to Divine Providence*, NC, TAN books, 2010.

De Mello, SJ, Anthony. *Sadhana, A Way to God: Christian Exercises in Eastern Form.* Garden City, NY: Image Books. 1984.

De Mello, SJ, Anthony. *Wellsprings: A Book of Spiritual Exercises.* Garden City, NJ: Image Books. 1986.

Downey, Michael. *Hope Begins Where Hope Begins,* NY, Orbis, 1998.

Foster, Richard. *Prayer: Finding the Heart's True Home.* San Francisco: Harper Collins, 1992.

Julian of Norwich, *Revelations of Divine Love,* Penguin Books. 1984.

Linn, Dennis, Sheila and Matthew. *Good Goats: Healing Our Image of God,* NJ: Paulist Press., 1993.

Llyewelyn, Robert. *All Shall Be Well: the Spirituality of Julian of Norwich for Today.* NJ: Paulist Press. 1985.

Martin, James. *My Life with the Saints, Between Heaven and Mirth*, Chicago, Loyola Press, 2006.

May, Gerald. *Addiction and Grace.* San Francisco: Harper San Francisco. 1991.

Muller, Wayne. *Sabbath: Finding Rest, Renewal, and Delight in Our Busy Lives,* NY, Bantam, 2000.

Muto, Susan. *Celebrating the Single Life: A Spirituality for Single Persons in Today's World.* NY: Crossroad. 1989.

Nouwen, Henri. *Reaching Out: The Three Movements of the Spiritual Life.* Garden City, NY: Image Books. 1986.

Powers, John. *A Spirituality of Compassion.* Mystic, CT: Twenty-Third Publications. 1988.

Puls, Joan. *A Spirituality of Compassion.* Mystic, CT: Twenty-Third Publications. 1988.

Rock, SJ, Leo P. *Making Friends with Yourself.* NY: Paulist Press. 1990.

Rolheiser, Ronald. *Holy Longing.* NY: Doubleday. 1999.

Sinetar, Marsha. *Ordinary People as Monks and Mystics: Lifestyles for Self-Discovery.* NY: Paulist Press. 1986.

St. Augustine. *City of God.* Marcus Dods, Trans. NY: Modern Library. 1993.

Confessions: A Modern English Version. Orleans, MA: Paraclete Press. 1986.

St. Francis de Sales. *Introduction to the Devout Life.* John Ryan, trans. NY: Image Books. 1989.

St. Francis of Assisi. *The Little Flowers of St. Francis: A Paraphrase.* Donald Demarcy. NY: Alba House. 1992.

St. Teresa of Avila. *Autobiography of St. Teresa of Avila.* E. Allison Peers, trans. NY: Doubleday. 1991.

St. Therese of Lisieux. *Story of a Soul, the Autobiography of St. Therese of Lisieux.* By John Clarke, ICS Publications, 1999.

Clarke, John. *St. Therese of Lisieux: Her Last Conversations*, Institute of Carmelite Studies Publications 1977.

Taylor, Jeremy. *Dream Work: Techniques for Discovering the Creative Power in Dreams.* NY: Paulist Press. 1983.

Wicks, Robert J. *Touching the Holy: Ordinariness, Self-esteem, and Friendship.* Notre Dame: Ave Maria. 1992.

Wuellmer, Flora. Slosson *Prayer and Our Bodies*, TN, The Upper Room, 1987.

Male Spirituality and Studies

Arnold, Patrick. Wildmen, *Warriors, and Kings: Masculine Spirituality and the Bible.* NY: Crossroads. 1992.

Bly, Robert. *Iron John: A Book About Men.* NY: Vintage. 1991.

Carmody, John. *Toward a Male Spirituality.* Mystic, CT: Twenty-Third Publications. 1992.

Keen, Sam. *Fire in the Belly: On Being Man.* NY: Bantam Books. 1992.

Rohr, Richard and Joseph Martos. *The Wild Man's Journey: Reflections on Male Spirituality.* Cincinnati, OH: St. Anthony Messenger Press. 1992.

Rohr, Richard. *Adam's Return: The Five Promises of Male Initiation*, NY, The Crossroads Publication Company, 2004.

Women's Spirituality

Kidd, Sue Monk. *The Secret Life of Bees*, NY, Penguin, 2003.

St. Teresa of Avila, *The Interior Castle Study Edition* Translator: Kieran Kavanaugh (Author), Translator: Otilio Rodriguez (Author), Prepared by: Kieran Kavanaugh (Editor), Prepared by: Carol Lisi (Editor) ICS Publications, 2010.

Harris, Maria. *Dance of the Spirit*, NY, Bantam, 1991.

Turpin, Joanne. *Women in Church History: 20 Stories for 20 Centuries*, Cincinatti, OH, St. Anthony Messenger Press, 2007.

Wolski, Conn, Joann, ED. *Women's Spirituality,* Mahwah, NJ, Paulist Press, 1996.

BIBLIOGRAPHY

Abbot, SJ, Walter, ed. *The Documents of Vatican II.* NY: Guild Press. 1966.

Angelus, Silesius. *The Cherrrubinic Wanderer.* The Classics of Western Spirituality. NY: Paulist Press. 1988.

Aidas, Chris. *Discernment: Seeking God in Every Situation.* NY: Living Flame Press. 1981.

Au, Wilke. *By Way of the Heart: Towards a Holistic Christian Spirituality.* NY/Mahwah: Paulist Press. 1989.

Barry, SJ, William A. *God and You: Prayer as a Personal Relationship.* NY: Paulist Press. 1987.

_____. *What do I Want in Prayer?* NY/Mahwah: Paulist Press. 1994.

Cameli, Lous; Miller, Robert; Weber, Gerard P. *A Sense of Direction.* Tabor Publishing. 1987.

Conroy, RSM, Maureen. *The Discerning Heart: Discovering a Personal God.* Chicago: Loyola University Press. 1993.

Cowan, CSJ, Marian; Futrell, SJ, John. *The Spiritual Exercises of St. Ignatius of Loyola: A Handbook for Directors.* Jesuit Educational Center for Human Development. Cambridge, MA. 1982.

De Mello, SJ, Anthony. *Sadhana: A Way to God.* Gujarat Sahitya Prakash, India. 1978.

DeThomasis, FSC, Louis. *Imagination: A Future for Religious Life.* Winona, MN: The Metanoia Group. 1992.

Donovan, Daniel. *What are They Saying About the Ministerial Priesthood?* NY: Paulist Press. 1982.

Dyckman, SNJM, Katherine Marie; Carroll, SSJ, Patrick. *Inviting the Mystic Supporting the Prophet.* NY: Paulist Press. 1981.

English, John J. *Choosing Life: The Significance of Personal History in Decision-Making.* NY: Paulist Press. 1978.

Farnam, Suzanne; Gill, Joseph; McLean, R. Taylor; Ward, Susan. *Listening Hearts: Discerning Call in Community.* Harrisburg, PA: Morehouse Publishing. 1991.

Finn, Virginia S. *Pilgrim in the Parish: A Spirituality for Lay Ministers.* NY: Paulist Press. 1986.

Fleming, SJ, David, ed. "Notes on the Spiritual Exercises of St. Ignatius of Loyola: the Best of the Review." St. Louis, MO. *Review for Religious.* 1981.

_____. *The Spiritual Exercises of St. Ignatius: A Literal Translation and a Contemporary Reading.* St. Louis, MO: Institute of Jesuit Sources. 1978.

_____. *A Contemporary Reading of the Spiritual Exercises: A Companion to St. Ignatius' Test.* St. Louis, MO: Institute of Jesuit Resources. 1980. C. 1978.

Fox, Matthew. *Original Blessing.* Santa Fe, NM: Bear. 1983.

Hakenwerth, SSM, Quentin. *Following Your Inner Call.* Chicago, IL: National Catholic Vocation Council. 1981.

Hart, Thomas N. *The Art of Christian Listening.* NY: Paulist Press. 1980.

Komonchak, Joseph A.; Colins, Mary; Lane, Dermot, eds. *The New Dictionary of Theology.* Wilmington, DE: Michael Glazier. 1991.

Lane, Dermot. *The Experience of God: An Invitation To Do Theology.* NY: Paulist Press. 1981.

Lane, CM, Thomas. *A Priesthood in Tune: Theological Reflections on Ministry.* Dublin. Columbia Press. 1993.

Larkin, OCarm, Ernest. *Silent Presence: Discernment as Process and Problems.* NJ: Dimension Books. 1981.

Leddy, Mary Joe. *Revealing Religious Life: Beyond the Liberal Model.* Mystic, CT: Twenty-Third Publications. 1990.

Lewis, Roy. *Choosing Your Career, Finding Your Vocation.* NY: Integration Books. Paulist Press. 1989.

Lozano, John. *Discipleship: Towards an Understanding of Religious Life.* Chicago, IL: Claret Center for Resources in Spirituality. 1980.

MacMurray, John. *Persons in Relation.* NY: Harper. 1957. Guildford Lectures. 1953 – 1954.

McKinney, OSB, Mary Benet. *Sharing Wisdom: a Process for Group Decision-Making.* Tabor Publishers.

Merkle, Judith A. *Committed By Choice: Religious Life Today.* Collegeville, MN: The Liturgical Press. 1992.

Mottola, Anthony, trans. *The Spiritual Exercises of St. Ignatius.* Garden City, NY: Doubleday and Co., Inc. 1963.

Neal, SNDdeN, Marie Augusta. *Catholic Sisters in Transition from the 1960's to the 1980's.* Wilmington, DE: Michael Glazier, Inc. 1984.

Nygren, David J. and Ukeritis, Miriam D. *The Future of Religious Orders in the United States: Transformation and Commitment.* Westport, CT: Praeger. 1994.

Osborne, Kenan B. *Priesthood: A History of Ordained Ministry in the Roman Catholic Church.* NY: Seabury Press. 1983.

____. *Sacramental Theology: A General Introduction.* NY: Paulist Press. 1988.

Pennington, M. Basil. *Called: New Thinking on Christian Vocation.* NY: Seabury Press. 1983.

____. *Centered Living: The Way of Centering Prayer.* Garden City, NY: Seabury Press. 1986.

Philibert, OP, Paul J. *Living in the Meantime: Concerning the Transformation of Religious Life.* NY/Mahwah: Paulist Press. 1994.

Rausch, Thomas P. *Priesthood Today: An Appraisal.* NY: Paulist Press. 1992.

Schneiders, Sandra Marie. *Beyond Patching: Faith and Feminism in the Catholic Church.* NY: Paulist Press. 1991.

_____. *New Wineskins.* NY: Paulist Press. 1986.

Seuss, Dr. *Oh, The Places You'll Go!* NY: Random House. 1990.

Shannon, William H. "Original Blessing: The Gift of the True Self." *The Way.* 30:1. 1990, p. 42.

Sweetser, SJ, Thomas; Holden, Carol Wisniewski. *Leadership in a Successful Parish.* NY: Harper and Row. 1987.

Sweetser, SJ, Thomas. *Successful Parishes: How They Meet the Challenge of Change.* Minneapolis, MN: Winston Press. 1983.

Sweetser, SJ, Thomas; Forester, Patricia M. *Transforming the Parish: Models for the Future.* Kansas City, MO: Sheed and Ward. 1993.

Teilard de Chardin, Pierre. *The Divine Milieu.* NY: Harper and Row, Perennial Library. 1960.

Tetlow, SJ, Joseph. *Choosing Christ in the World: Direction of the Spiritual Exercise of St. Ignatius According to Annotations 18 and 19.* St. Louis, MO: The Institute of Jesuit Sources. 1989.

Veltri, SJ, J. *Orientations.* Vol. 1. (A collection of helps for prayer.) Guelph, ONT: Loyola House. 1979.

Wiederkehr, Macrina. *A Tree Full of Angels.* San Francisco: Harper and Row: 1988.

Wolff, Pierre. *Discernment: The Art of Choosing Well.* Missouri: Triumph Books. 1993.

About the Author

Sr. Kathleen Bryant is a Religious Sister of Charity. For twenty-one years, Sr. Kathleen served as a Talent Scout for God as a Vocation Director for the Archdiocese of Los Angeles. Sr. Kathleen grew up as a California beach girl who entered the convent in 1967 and served as a missionary in Africa for 5 years before responding to the call in vocation ministry. Presently, Sr. Kathleen ministers in the field of spirituality as a facilitator, retreat director, spiritual director and workshop presenter. Sr. Kathleen earned a Doctor of Ministry Degree from the Graduate Theological Foundation and a Master Degree in Spirituality from the University of San Francisco. She has authored numerous articles and books and has presented workshops and retreats in Australia, Ireland, Africa, and throughout the United States. Sr. Kathleen presently serves on the RSC Regional Leadership Team for California. Among her passions are connecting people with God in a digital world, teaching discernment and prayer, and working for the abolition of human trafficking and slavery.